M000014669

Slaying
GRACE

Slaying GRACE

A Guide for a Graceful and Grace-filled Life

Nicole R. Reed

MYND MATTERS

Copyright © 2021 by Nicole Reed

All rights reserved. No part of this publication may be reproduced, stored or transmitted in any form or by any means, electronic, mechanical, photocopying, recording, scanning, or otherwise without written permission from the publisher. It is illegal to copy this book, post it to a website, or distribute it by any other means without permission.

Nicole Reed asserts the moral right to be identified as the author of this work. Nicole Reed has no responsibility for the persistence or accuracy of URLs for external or third-party Internet websites referred to in this publication and does not guarantee that any content on such websites is, or will remain, accurate or appropriate. Designations used by companies to distinguish their products are often claimed as trademarks. All brand names and product names used in this book and on its cover are trade names, service marks, trademarks and registered trademarks of their respective owners. The publisher and *Slaying Grace* are not associated with any product or vendor mentioned in this book.

None of the companies referenced within the book have endorsed the book.

Books may be purchased in bulk quantity and/or special sales by contacting the publisher.

Published by Mynd Matters Publishing
715 Peachtree Street NE
Suites 100 & 200
Atlanta, GA 30308
www.myndmatterspublishing.com

ISBN-13: 978-1-953307-98-9 (pbk)
e-ISBN: 978-1-953307-99-6

FIRST EDITION

To the late, great Dr. Yvonne M. Patterson,
You showed me grace and taught me how to extend grace
towards myself. You ignited the spark that started my
spiritual and wellness journey. Though the loss of you in
the physical realm was devastating, I recognize that your
spirit lives on.

I am enough.

Contents

Introduction

"Do the best you can until you know better. Then, when you know better, do better."
–Dr. Maya Angelou

The Hall of Mirrors at Versailles! This is what heaven must look like. Gilded, glorious, grand. As I glide the length of the gallery in my regal, amethyst-hued ball gown, the visual feast of crystal chandeliers, mirrors, and sculptures require my complete silence. I take it all in. Every nook of the French palace is art. "Opulent" is rarely a part of my vocabulary, yet I struggle to conjure another word to surpass it because I do not feel the word does this space justice.

Why am I dressed to the nines in one of the most famous rooms in the world? I am not there with throngs of tourists, but rather heading to a private dining salon for the ultimate culinary fantasy—an exclusive dinner party orchestrated by the *Michelin Man* himself, Alain Ducasse.

The sublime eight-course, wine-paired dinner was inspired by meals hosted for the eighteenth century royal court. The scrumptious food should have been the main highlight, yet I could not stop marveling over the perfectly crafted centerpieces, exquisite China and glassware, personalized details, and the military precision service.

Etiquette and protocol excite me. There, I said it. Alas, to have been a fly on the walls of Versailles during King Louis XIV's reign. Not to witness the depravity, snobbery, or whims of a tyrant, though that would have been more entertaining than modern reality television. Experiencing Versailles during her rebirth, as a home and court for a monarch, would have been breathtaking, yet my focus would have been on the ceremonial customs and rituals assigned to every aspect of daily life. Rigid rules regarding dining, dressing, and manners were strictly enforced and provided structure.

"DURING
THE SEVENTEENTH CENTURY, IN FRANCE,
MANNERS BECAME A POLITICAL ISSUE. KING
LOUIS XIV AND HIS PREDECESSORS, IN
COLLECTING TOGETHER THE NOBILITY OF
FRANCE TO LIVE WITH THE SOVEREIGN AT
VERSAILLES, INSTITUTED A SORT OF SCHOOL OF
MANNERS.

AT THE PALACE, THE COURTIERS LIVED UNDER
THE DESPOTIC SURVEILLANCE OF THE KING,
AND UPON THEIR GOOD BEHAVIOUR, THEIR
DEFERENCE, AND THEIR OBSERVANCE OF
ETIQUETTE THEIR WHOLE CAREERS DEPENDED."

MARGARET VISSER
THE RITUALS OF DINNER
THE ORIGINS, EVOLUTION, ECCENTRICITIES, AND MEANING OF TABLE MANNERS
GROVE WEINDENFELD, 1991

It is my belief that this manner of über-etiquette and protocol is at the top of the rigidity spectrum by which etiquette is measured, though the debauchery and backstabbing throughout the halls of Versailles exposed the absence of good manners. All societies have social ranks and codes of conduct. Some are prim and formalized, oral and sacred, or fluid and natural. Allow me to be your guide and advisor for a more modernized and inclusive approach to decorum.

* * *

Passion plus purpose inspired me to create this modern etiquette road map from a wholly Black American voice. Even as a modern, fiercely independent woman in the "Me-Too" era, I swoon over Netflix's diversely cast *Bridgerton*, which is a British historical romance series chronicling the high society marriage market of the 1800s. It is replete with lavish balls, exquisite attire, chivalry, and, of course, the fairytale ending.

My timeline for completing the book was expedited after a friend forwarded me a flyer titled "Martin Luther King Weekend Freedom To Twerk Party." The slain Civil Rights leader's head was transposed on a neck dripping with gold chains, and several scantily clad, twerk-ready women were positioned around him. This galvanized me to continue my efforts and to do my part in "Saving Grace."

Social media has amplified and desensitized the public to unsocial behaviors such as bullying, disrespect, and cruelty. No segment of society has escaped the dizzying confusion of what is socially acceptable behavior. World leaders berate and mock objectors. "Telling it like it is" and "not biting your tongue" are valued over tactfulness and, at times, the truth. The capacity to be shocked has disintegrated due to the twenty-four-hour news cycles and social media's bombardment of embarrassing and private moments, not intended for public consumption. If your desire is to stay above the fray while maintaining your sanity, what can you do? If buying a private island without Internet access is out of the question, communication tools and practice are needed to thrive in this world gracefully.

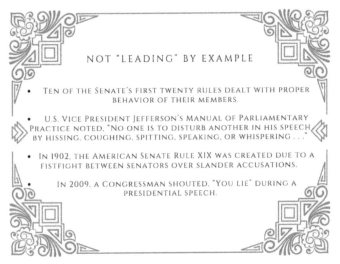

NOT "LEADING" BY EXAMPLE

- TEN OF THE SENATE'S FIRST TWENTY RULES DEALT WITH PROPER BEHAVIOR OF THEIR MEMBERS.

- U.S. VICE PRESIDENT JEFFERSON'S MANUAL OF PARLIAMENTARY PRACTICE NOTED, "NO ONE IS TO DISTURB ANOTHER IN HIS SPEECH BY HISSING, COUGHING, SPITTING, SPEAKING, OR WHISPERING . . ."

- IN 1902, THE AMERICAN SENATE RULE XIX WAS CREATED DUE TO A FISTFIGHT BETWEEN SENATORS OVER SLANDER ACCUSATIONS.

- IN 2009, A CONGRESSMAN SHOUTED, "YOU LIE" DURING A PRESIDENTIAL SPEECH.

In 2007, work first took me to Japan, which I found gloriously refined and dignified. With over thirty million inhabitants, one must have a strong appreciation for the country's orderliness, cleanliness, and muted elegance. For example, the Japanese tea ceremony (*sadō/chadō*) is intertwined with *omotenashi*, which means to wholeheartedly look after guests. Therefore, it was no surprise I received best-in-class service throughout my stay. People were not putting on an act or performing at high levels to acquire tips. Gratuities were typically declined and never anticipated. Social media was not the Pandora's box that it is today; therefore, avoidance of reputational damage was not at play. Authentic people-focused service was embedded into the culture. Shortly after my visit to Japan, I traveled to India and Thailand and found their hospitality industries just as customer-centric.

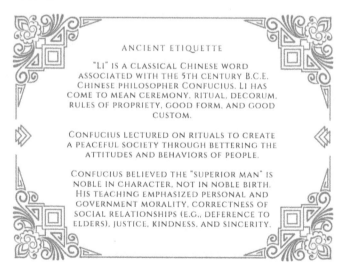

ANCIENT ETIQUETTE

"LI" IS A CLASSICAL CHINESE WORD ASSOCIATED WITH THE 5TH CENTURY B.C.E. CHINESE PHILOSOPHER CONFUCIUS. LI HAS COME TO MEAN CEREMONY, RITUAL, DECORUM, RULES OF PROPRIETY, GOOD FORM, AND GOOD CUSTOM.

CONFUCIUS LECTURED ON RITUALS TO CREATE A PEACEFUL SOCIETY THROUGH BETTERING THE ATTITUDES AND BEHAVIORS OF PEOPLE.

CONFUCIUS BELIEVED THE "SUPERIOR MAN" IS NOBLE IN CHARACTER, NOT IN NOBLE BIRTH. HIS TEACHING EMPHASIZED PERSONAL AND GOVERNMENT MORALITY, CORRECTNESS OF SOCIAL RELATIONSHIPS (E.G., DEFERENCE TO ELDERS), JUSTICE, KINDNESS, AND SINCERITY.

At etiquette and protocol school, I learned manners are the guiding principles of putting people at ease, not embarrassing others, and being selfless. Etiquette is defined as the set of rules by which society lives. A parable used to illustrate the difference is a visiting dignitary drinking from a finger bowl and the royal host mirroring the action to avoid embarrassing his guest. This illustrates good manners on the part of the host, yet drinking out of the finger bowl is not proper "etiquette."

* * *

Retracing my steps, I recognize I was destined to follow a path in etiquette and ethics. Remember the good-nature kid in school who was a straight-A student, crossing guard, church usher, bookworm, always coloring inside the lines, an omnivert. That was me. The born diplomat and "box checker," which is how former First Lady Michelle Obama described herself during her book tour for her autobiography, *Becoming*. Back then, my fellow classmates might have used the terms *nerd*, *old-fashioned*, or *brown-noser* in lieu of *diplomat*; nevertheless, I do not hold that against them.

Where are my manners? Let me introduce myself and explain the importance of a book on social graces and etiquette from a Black American vantage point.

From birth, I was reared by my maternal grandparents, who migrated to the Greater Cincinnati area from Georgia in the 1940s, after my grandfather was honorably discharged from the Army. He spent decades pastoring in the Church of God in Christ (COGIC) denomination, while my grandmother moved up the evangelical ranks to become the regional president of the Home & Foreign Missions for Southwest Ohio.

My mother and father were teens when my siblings and I were born, and they depended on our grandparents to care for us. My grandfather was a man of quiet strength, and his wife (whom we affectionately called "Mama") was the dominant force in the lives of those who met her. My grandmother's side hustle was being an in-home childcare provider, and her primary mission was Jesus's earthly enforcer.

As the story goes, and from what I witnessed, once she was saved, secular activities such as profanity, drinking alcohol, smoking, and cursing were prohibited in her household. I even recall being reprimanded for popping my fingers. Not once did I see her partake in any of the aforementioned activities or wear anything other than a skirt or dress. My sister and I accompanied her while she evangelized outside of local supermarkets. She laid hands on and anointed with oil neighbors who recognized us, as well as strangers "standing in the need of prayer."

Sunday's best was our uniform as we attended church throughout the week, visited regional congregations, and played hostesses when my grandmother held meetings with her fellow hat-clad missionaries. Our lives revolved around home, church, and school, the latter being my utmost favorite. Mama and Pawpaw died when I was in elementary school, and I started junior high school living with my paternal grandmother. Like my other grandparents and many northern Black Americans, she had migrated to Ohio from a small town in Alabama.

Though she was a cook by trade, she missed her calling as an Army drill sergeant. Cinderella would have pitied me. Without prompting, I was required to dust and vacuum the entire house every Saturday. Dishes were cleaned and stored immediately after meals. Clothes were neatly folded or hung in the closet. Beds were always made and, barring extreme illness, sleeping-in was not tolerated. And since I had very few privileges, such as having a phone in my room, I was forced to have coded conversations with my friends in front of an audience and watch old-fashion television shows like *Murder, She Wrote*.

Each school day, she gave a quick, visual inspection under the guise of locking up behind me, which she needed to do because she never provided me with a house key. Allowance was a foreign word, so I held down multiple part-time jobs while remaining an excellent student. No-fuss holidays, birthdays, and limited visitors were the norm. My grandmother's rigidity, at times, was a mild annoyance, yet as I reflect on my teen years, I recognize I am wired for structure and organization.

Why am I providing insights into my beginnings, you ask? For two reasons: first, to explain how my social values and habits were formed. Second, to demonstrate that, in no way, am I looking down my nose at anyone. Though I was not born with the proverbial silver spoon, I cultivated an appreciation for refinement and fine dining. Throughout my life, grandparents, guardian angels, church moms, work mentors, and friends have guided me along the way. That is why I am committed to equipping others with the tools needed to navigate any situation. Trust me, there are days in which I am moments away from being a raving madwoman, ready to pounce on the next inconsiderate or annoying person. I am a work in progress, too, and I am excited about all the new things I have yet to discover.

* * *

A finance degree was the safe option I took in college, believing it was what I needed to succeed. My love for history would only be recognized with a minor. After graduation, I spent two decades working for Fortune 500 companies where I was exposed to a myriad of cultures in the form of world travel: from Austria to Australia, Canada to China, Ireland to Italy, South Africa to South Korea, and beyond. When my professional journeys stopped, my personal missions kept me going around the globe. In London, I completed my formal etiquette and protocol education with the highest level of distinction, at a school founded by a former member of the Royal Household of Her Majesty, The Queen.

I have dined overlooking the Sphinx, attended the most exclusive masquerade ball in Venice, and partied in Singapore with the world's best chefs. I have experienced unparalleled hospitality at a modest family home in Jordan, entertained business colleagues, and formed lifelong friendships with the kindest people in the world. My formal etiquette training, decades of international business experience, years of global exploration, coupled with a lifetime of navigating multiple cultures provides me with a unique and comprehensive awareness of social and business norms. Is there a place for etiquette in modern society? My answer is a resounding "yes," and that is where I come in.

* * *

For some, "etiquette" conjures images of the economically elite or aristocratic classes due to chivalry, sophistication, and decorum being historically associated with specific groups. The conscious and subconscious rules around what is "proper" are steeped in bias and, at times, excuse or cover up appalling behavior.

No group has a monopoly on good manners, and proper etiquette is not one-size fits all. I like to think of the knowledge in this book as manageable manners "morsels" or "snacks," not a comprehensive manual. This guide will serve as a refresher of the nature of etiquette, explain how social graces are accessible to everyone, then arm you with tools, techniques, and recommendations to aid you in your quest for a life filled with grace.

Though the guidance within these pages is beneficial to all audiences, you may notice nuances within the Black community being addressed. This is my frame of reference, and I affirm some of these stories can be insightful to other groups.

* * *

Let me recount a recent interaction with a stranger. Chatting up my Uber driver, I learned he was retired and enjoyed driving to keep himself occupied. He revealed he was having his large family over for the summer holiday and exclaimed his daughter's guest from a previous gathering was not allowed back in his house.

He explained that the young man, approximately in his early twenties, brought spirits that only he drank and had the audacity to take it with him when he left. I inquired if he had voiced his concerns to the young man. His response to the situation was to mention the city's open container laws, to which the young man responded he could handle himself.

This scenario has been played out before in homes where I have been a guest. This was a teachable moment, and I believe the young man did not recognize he was being an ungracious guest in many ways. First, he did not show gratitude for the invitation by bringing a gift for the host. Instead, he brought his own drink, which infers that the host would be ungracious by not providing drinks, or that the drinks would be unappetizing. His next transgression was he hoarded liquor and dismissed the host's advice on the local law.

When I was this young man's age, I was at university in the late nineties, prior to the explosion of the Internet. My college roommate's mom sent us on an errand to purchase a thank you gift for a professor. She suggested dark liquor, so we ventured to the small-town center to see what we could find.

That evening, my roomie reported back the details of our purchase. Her mom's response was, "You can't give him that wino-sized bottle of liquor." Unbeknownst to us, size matters when gifting alcohol! We were barely over the drinking age and did not know the proper etiquette. I still giggle at this memory. Occasions such as these provide prior generations the opportunity to teach proper etiquette. Please note the professor, in all likelihood, would have graciously received the "wino" sized gift and recognized the spirit in which the gift was being given. Good manners on his part, yet not proper etiquette for the gift.

Just like my roommate's mother, I aim to meet people where they are and catch them up on how to handle themselves in every situation. But I also realize the advice within these pages will not resonate with everyone, and that is okay. Some of my recommendations may be perceived as common sense, but as you read, keep in mind that "common sense is not all that common" and not everyone has a role model.

* * *

Grace is such a powerful and multi-faceted word. *Merriam-Webster* lists many definitions for grace: "to confer dignity or honor," "a virtue coming from God," "a sense of propriety," and "a state of sanctification." Coming of age in an evangelical household, saying grace before a meal happened automatically. Now "grace" has become the "it" word for the modern spiritualist movement. There is no shortage of inspirational quotes with the word, such as my favorite, "Grace will take you places hustling can't." Tune into Oprah's *Super Soul Sunday* and it is part of the vocabulary of every guest.

The original title for this book was *Saving Grace*, and it revealed itself to me one morning as I was waking up. Given the religious connotation of this title, I explored other options. Next, *Grace Codes* was voted down because some may liken it to the Black Codes passed by Confederate states, which, in essence, told Black people what they could and could not do. I landed on *Slaying Grace* because, for me, the title represents a modernized twist on manners.

The incomparable Dr. Maya Angelou said, *"Grace is like a lake of drinkable water right outside your door."* Grace is within reach and easily obtainable. Please join me on this grace-filled journey!

Golden Rules

"I respect myself and insist upon it from everybody.
And because I do it, I then respect everybody, too.
–Dr. Maya Angelou

As the late lyricist Tupac Shakur eloquently said, *"Follow the rules or follow the fools." Slaying Grace* delves into an array of topics, yet there are some rules that are universally imperative, no matter the situation. These are the ground rules I regard as non-negotiable.

TREAT ME RIGHT

Shu (Self-Reflection) *"What you do not desire for yourself, do not do to others"* is the Confucian concept of reciprocity or mutual considerateness in all actions. In Western society, we use expressions such as *"treat people how you would want to be treated"* or *"do unto others as you would have them do unto you."* I take this rule one step further. People should be treated how "they" want to be treated.

I have friends who prefer to receive news concisely and bluntly while others appreciate a subtle or delicate approach. Everyone should be treated with respect, with a tailored delivery based on their preferences. Another example is when friends recognize I have an aversion to drinking adult beverages out of red plastic cups. In response, they graciously provide me with glassware, while everyone else merrily and unsophisticatedly expand their carbon footprint. Just kidding! Sort of!

Another story I want to share is from my early corporate days. I was part of a team that traveled together extensively. A particularly quirky, straight-laced colleague, who was a proud member of the Titanic Historical Society and Queen Mary Association, was convinced to join others at a rowdy hockey game. Knowing his proclivities and personality, the team managed to find a concession stand that served wine in a proper cup and brought it to him in the stands, while those around him chugged beers.

Personal touches such as these are the highest expressions of making others feel included and welcomed. Even for occasions when you are entering unknown territory, use how you want to be treated as a gauge, and then adjust once you learn more about the individuals you are interacting with.

SAGE

The animal kingdom is teeming with veterans who instinctively serve as protectors, nurturers, and teachers for the next generation. Prior to the modern information era, elders were the dominant source of knowledge and the guardians of traditions.

First, allow me to clarify that age and wisdom are not always in alignment. Though "respect your elders" has been wired into my brain since my youth, I recognize that this expression may imply blind loyalty based on a person's age. That is why I prefer the use of the title "sage." My interpretation of a sage is someone with experience, who is willing to guide others through unwritten rules and provide perspective on what worked in the past. Though technology has its advantages, there are lessons that cannot be learned with the click of a button.

During my time in a small town in Louisiana, I had the pleasure of forming a close relationship with a formidable woman who is now in her eighties named Mrs. Z. Her community holds her in high esteem. For example, when young men came into her store with their underwear visible, she asked them to pull up their pants. They complied without protest. Though her demeanor and sharp tongue come across as harsh, I believe they are coming from a place of tough love mixed with frustration.

Another noteworthy incident occurred when a customer came into her store holding a bedazzled "pimp cup" while yelling into his phone. Her response to him forcing his phone conversation on everyone was, "What are you celebrating, poverty?" This would not have been my recommended response. Others may argue this was respectability politics, which I do not believe was the case.

Her desire for him to modify his behavior had nothing to do with how other groups would perceive him.

In her youth, Mrs. Z found a way to get a ride to an HBCU in Louisiana because the college in her town did not allow Black Americans to enroll. Eventually, she earned her undergraduate and graduate degrees, then pursued a Ph.D. She created a career for herself in teaching, and then she and her late husband started a business that has helped her family thrive to this day. She has earned the respect of her family and community. Mrs. Z and I do not always agree, yet I recognize she has been where I am and where I want to eventually be. She is a wise elder and sage who I respect tremendously.

R.E.S.P.E.C.T.

Speaking of respect... Historically, the use of honorifics, such as Mr., Mrs., Dr., Captain, and Your Honor, were used as a courtesy or to convey respect for a social or professional superior. I witnessed firsthand the extensive honorific system in Japan. Though Japanese society is heavily hierarchical, routine dialogue expresses a level of respect and politeness. After receiving a crash course on the use of the Japanese honorific "San," I was able to address my Tokyo-based colleagues and new acquaintances with the respect due to them based on the cultural norms of that society.

As contemporary societies become less formal and more egalitarian, some honorific systems show signs of eroding. As a staunch advocate for the use of honorifics and titles, I am using this platform to encourage their revival, especially when addressing elders, strangers, and specific professionals (e.g., doctors, judges, etc.).

During a 1990s talk show appearance, a young lady addressed Dr. Angelou as "Maya" when asking a question. Immediately, Dr. Angelou corrected her and said, "Thank you. And first, I'm Ms. Angelou. I'm not Maya. I'm sixty-two years old. I've lived so long and tried so hard that a young woman like you, or any other, has no license to come up to me and call me by my first name." Do not take the liberty of addressing elders by their first name unless they grant you permission, even those you do not hold in high esteem. I would not call a friend's crabby grandfather by his first name. Think of it as a demonstration of *your* politeness or respect for how others want to be treated.

This also applies to the use of *ma'am* and *sir*, which in the United States, are more regionally expected, particularly in the Deep South. In his essay "Racial Etiquette: The Racial Customs and Rules of Racial Behavior in Jim Crow America," Dr. Ronald L.F. Davis explains the intent of Jim Crow etiquette was for Black Americans to demonstrate their inferiority to Whites by actions, words, and manners.[1] For example, no matter

---

[1] Ronald L. F. Davis, Ph.D., "Racial Etiquette: The Racial Customs and Rules of Racial Behavior in Jim Crow America."
https://web.archive.org/web/20040203140654/
http://www.jimcrowhistory.org/resources/lessonplans/hs_es_etiquette.htm

their age, Black Americans were called "boy" or "girl," yet were required to address Whites, including at times children, as "Mister" and "Miss."

The majority of the U.S. Black population live in the South, and most northern Blacks were part of or have ties to the Great Migration from the rural southern states, the pinnacle of Jim Crow segregationist statutes. It is no wonder there are unwritten rules regarding the use of honorifics in Black homes and churches I have encountered because there was a time, in recent memory, when it was customary to exclude Blacks from this form of social respect.

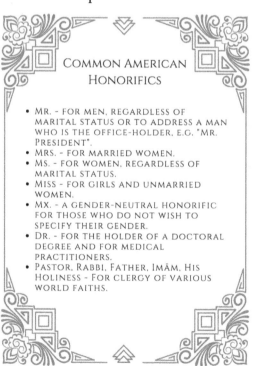

COMMON AMERICAN HONORIFICS

- MR. - FOR MEN, REGARDLESS OF MARITAL STATUS OR TO ADDRESS A MAN WHO IS THE OFFICE-HOLDER, E.G. "MR. PRESIDENT".
- MRS. - FOR MARRIED WOMEN.
- MS. - FOR WOMEN, REGARDLESS OF MARITAL STATUS.
- MISS - FOR GIRLS AND UNMARRIED WOMEN.
- MX. - A GENDER-NEUTRAL HONORIFIC FOR THOSE WHO DO NOT WISH TO SPECIFY THEIR GENDER.
- DR. - FOR THE HOLDER OF A DOCTORAL DEGREE AND FOR MEDICAL PRACTITIONERS.
- PASTOR, RABBI, FATHER, IMĀM, HIS HOLINESS - FOR CLERGY OF VARIOUS WORLD FAITHS.

WHO YOU CALLING A . . .

Let's face it—we all use profanity, especially when stubbing our toe, describing a reality TV star we love to hate, locking our keys in the car, or being cut off in traffic. Author Mark Twain aptly said, "Under certain circumstances, profanity provides a relief denied even to prayer." While researching the topic, I was surprised by the number of articles extolling the virtues of profanity. Some studies say it builds camaraderie, shows honesty, and demonstrates passion.

On the opposite end of the spectrum, in her book *Swearing is Good for You: The Amazing Science of Bad Language*, author and artificial intelligence researcher Emma Byrne writes, "If you ask people what they think about swearing, they tend to insist that it diminishes the speaker's credibility and persuasiveness."[2]

In the United States, free speech is an inalienable right that I fully support and embrace. However, when profanity is used as a weapon to bully, demean, and intimidate, that is where I draw the line on its use. As I am writing this book, journalist Gayle King is being crucified on social media for asking questions about a celebrity's past in the wake of his death. Civility was thrown out the window as profanity-laced,

---

[2] *Swearing is Good for You: The Amazing Science of Bad Language*, February 26, 2019 by W. W. Norton Company, author and artificial intelligence researcher Emma Byrne.

misogynistic, and threatening comments filled public forums. This is never okay. Eventually many of the famous perpetrators apologized and did the common social media backpedaling. The care and time that these artists take to craft lyrics should be mirrored when addressing opposing views on social platforms.

> *"When you know you are of worth, you don't have to raise your voice, you don't have to become rude, you don't have to become vulgar; you just are."*
> **—Dr. Maya Angelou**

YOU MUST MAKE HASTE

While in New York, enjoying the spectacular Tina Turner Broadway musical, my eyes became fixated on the throngs of people being escorted to their seat after the rise of the curtain. As a proponent of shutting the doors and ushering late arrivers to the standing room section until intermission, I admittedly was vexed. My companion and I had purposefully made post-show dinner reservations and selected a hotel less than two blocks away, so we would be on time, not only to avoid missing any part of the show, but also out of respect for the performers and our fellow patrons. On more than one occasion, I have jumped out an NYC cab and sprinted to the theater in heels to make it to the theater on time. If ever I was be late, I would be bummed, yet not offended if I had to wait in the back. Keeping people waiting is not my forte, and I value when others show me the same courtesy.

The phrase "Colored People's Time" (CPT) infers people of color, particularly those we identify as Black, are habitually late. Whether this stereotype is true or if our absence is more noticeable has been and will continue to be debated by greater minds than mine. Friends who are alums of Historically Black Colleges & Universities (HBCUs) said they were schooled in the belief that "early is on time, on time is late, and late is unacceptable." Since Blacks, especially in the Western world, are a culture within a dominant culture, this lesson is imperative, and I want to reiterate it.

- Plan to be early to everything: weddings, job interviews, concerts, and critical meetings.

- Perform reconnaissance. This should include inquiring about the parking and sign-in process days prior. On the day of, arrive in the general vicinity, at least, one hour early to visually understand the logistics. If you have time to exhaust, settle into a nearby coffee shop to gather your thoughts for the meeting or event.

- For business meetings, arrive early in order to get prime seating, which is near the person chairing the meeting or within eyesight of the highest-ranking individual.

MEG ONLI, ASSOCIATE CURATOR OF THE MIT LIST VISUAL ARTS CENTER EXHIBIT TITLED 'COLORED PEOPLE'S TIME,' STATES THAT CPT "IS SIMULTANEOUSLY PERCEIVED AS A JOKE WITHIN THE BLACK COMMUNITY AND AS A PERFORMANCE THAT ALLOWS AN INDIVIDUAL TO EXIST WITHIN A TEMPORALITY CREATED BY THEMSELVES. THE PHRASE COMES TO FUNCTION AS A LINGUISTIC TOOL FOR PEOPLE OF COLOR TO CONTROL THEIR OWN TEMPORALITY EVEN WHEN PLACED WITHIN THE CONSTRUCT OF WESTERN TIME."

BE YOURSELF

Unlike *Bridgerton*, I do not believe chastity and honor are related. Respectability correlates with how you treat others. As the saying goes, "every angel has a past; every devil has a future." Embrace your past as much as your future. Today, we live in a cancel culture that has a double-edged sword. It calls to the carpet those less-tolerant people in our current society, as well as interprets and shines a light on every transgression ever made. It's hard to be your authentic self for fear of misinterpretation.

With that said, love who you are and bring your whole self to the table. This book is not recommending that you put on airs or start drinking a cup of tea with your pinky finger protruding, which, by the way, is not proper form. I have a visceral reaction when I hear the phrase "good family." It implies expectations are higher for those with affluence or devout religious backgrounds. Education, money, and influence do not automatically equate to having class or good manners. Etiquette and social graces are about behaviors, not belongings or status. Let your actions speak for you.

TRIGGER WARNING

One of the most misused expressions in the English language includes the phase "they made me." Unless you are physically overpowered, brainwashed, or threatened, it is rare for someone to "make" you do anything. I understand we all have triggers, and there are those that know which buttons to push, yet the choice is yours. For example, think about the annoying boy in grade school. You can choose to yell at him, play nice, or ignore him. It is tempting to fight crazy with crazy. Remember you are a highly evolved being, capable of maintaining your composure in the most uncomfortable of situations. It is your finger on the trigger. You have the power.

EXPRESS YOURSELF

Smiles, hugs, and handshakes are the universal cues for friendliness in the United States because they show interest, are welcoming, or put someone at ease. Studies by college researchers revealed the eyes offers the most robust indication of emotions, more than other areas of the face, such as the mouth.[3] This bodes well in a world of face coverings and masks.

Eye contact, waving, thumbs up, and uncrossing arms are just a few business norms to compensate when you cannot speak. Winking, a head nod, or tipping the hat are a few playful ways to acknowledge others. Make your words and tone count. Go the extra mile and be more expressive!

KNOW WHEN AND HOW TO APOLOGIZE

Apologizing or accepting an apology is difficult. Those wanting to apologize do not want to come off as insincere or as if they fear rejection. Receiving apologies are hard because people do not want to appear as if they are condoning the behavior, especially if the feelings of being slighted are still fresh. The benefits of an apology are countless. Not only does an apology demonstrate concern for the other party, but it can also mend relationships, provide closure, or ignite healing for the damaged party.

Someone once said I cut people so quickly, they don't bleed. Admittedly, I do tend to phase people out of my life, typically, for numerous small transgressions that I

---

[3] Stephen D'Angelo, Eye Expressions Offer a Glimpse Into the Evolution of Emotion, April 13, 2017, https://news.cornell.edu/stories/2017/04/eye-expressions-offer-glimpse-evolution-emotion.

allow to build up. Then, I reach a point where I feel a relationship with this person is no longer necessary. My nature to be accommodating is a major contributing factor to the buildup. Apologies, though appreciated, are fruitless once I've reached my capacity to pour energy into this person.

This brings me to my first point about an apology. The purpose of an apology is not redemption for the transgressor, nor should the assumption be made that the apology will be accepted. If an apology is not sincere or issued just to appease the other party, then do not bother.

My friend Tasha asked for my advice regarding a situation she was in with another friend. Tasha explained that she did not volunteer to throw a friend a baby shower. Now she was receiving the cold shoulder from the mom-to-be. She did not feel that she needed to apologize because she believed she did nothing wrong, and I concurred. My instincts told me Tasha wanted to salvage the friendship; otherwise, she would not have asked for my opinion. I advised her to go with the statement of fact approach versus apologizing.

"Sheila, I feel there has been tension between us for the past several weeks, and I want to clear the air. I am getting the impression you believe I have slighted you, and if so, I wanted to let you know that wasn't the intent." In this narrative, Tasha is stating a fact, which is she did not intend to slight anyone. Yet she is acknowledging the other person's feelings. This approach will, at a minimum, get the conversation going without apologizing or the need to assume blame.

If you wronged someone deliberately or unintentionally, the respectable course of action is to issue an apology. Depending on the severity of the offense, the apology can take many forms — flowers with a note, dinner, a greeting card, email, phone call, and most preferably, face-to-face. The expression "my bad" is like nails on a chalkboard to me. This flippant expression does not constitute an apology and is an avoidance technique. For property losses, you must apologize and make the person whole by replacing the item or paying the insurance deductible. Do not make excuses such as "That thing was so old. Why should I have to pay to replace it?" Show some grace.

CLEANLINESS IS NEXT TO GODLINESS

I must admit I am a tad neurotic when it comes to organizing and cleaning. I find it extremely therapeutic. Being tidy is in my nature, and it was further ingrained by my paternal grandmother. As I mentioned earlier, my grandmother ran a tight ship. We resided in a predominantly Black neighborhood in Cincinnati. Our home was modest, yet immaculate. As her friend, co-worker, and neighbor Mrs. Lucille always exclaimed, "You can eat off the floor" at our house.

Autumn tones provided warmth throughout the

first level. I avoided wearing socks because I loved the way the plush burnt orange carpet felt under my feet. The large floor model console TV with a built-in 8-track player was in pristine condition, though, at the time, it was over twenty years old. Visitors, besides my grandmother's younger siblings, were few and infrequent; nonetheless, my grandmother made sure her home stayed ready, so she would not have to get ready.

Recently, I was listening to the *1619* podcast, an audio series on how slavery transformed America. Its creator, the *New York Times* journalist Nikole Hannah-Jones, recounted how her Aunt Charlotte, a woman who wore high heels until she was in her nineties, always kept her house very neat, including plastic over the furniture. As Ms. Hannah-Jones describes, "It was very important for her, at all times, to appear respectable."[4] She attributed this to her aunt Charlotte not being treated with respect during her formative years growing up in the Jim Crow South.

I am not advocating a return to the dreaded plastic furniture coverings that saved many couches from the eighties Jheri Curl. What I am encouraging is maintaining a constant welcoming environment in all spaces in which we have ownership and responsibility.

---

[4] Nikole Hannah-Jones, podcast audio, *1619*: "Episode 2: The Economy That Slavery Built," August 30, 2019. https://www.nytimes.com/2019/08/23/podcasts/1619-slavery-annive rsary.html

Years ago, I noticed a friend's apartment and car were always a mess. I would arrive for a weekend visit, and she would have to put a load in the washer in order for me to have clean sheets and towels. Once, she even said, "I wish it would rain, so my car would get cleaned." I fired back, "Would the rain wash out these fast-food wrappers and clutter on the backseat?" Though she always knew the details of my arrival, her home was never in the proper state to receive guests. Eventually, I stopped accepting invitations to stay at her place and stayed at a hotel.

Shaman Durek spoke about a similar situation on his podcast *Ancient Wisdom Today*. He recounted a time when he refused to ride in a friend's "trashy" car. He went so far as to call an Uber, though they were going to and from the same location.[5] His "how dare you invite me into this space" attitude mirrors mine, though his depiction is more comical.

Being in disorganized spaces is unwelcoming, unsettling, and distracting. You cannot be a gracious host and should never permit others into your space when it is in disarray. Hire someone and set a reoccurring schedule to have your home and car cleaned.

Now that these matters are settled, let us carry on.

---

[5] Shaman Durek, interview with Jasmine Aten, *Ancient Wisdom Today* audio podcast, "Invite In the Magick," April 25, 2019. https://podcasts.apple.com/us/podcast/cxxiv-invite-in-the-magick-jasmine-aten

Don't Ask, Don't Tell

You may not control all the events that happen to you,
but you can decide not to be reduced by them.
–Dr. Maya Angelou

I am such a private person, a friend nicknamed me "The Vault." As an omnivert, also called a social introvert, I prefer not to broadcast my business, pry, or succumb to meddlesome people. This is not an attempt to be mysterious. Although I lived under her roof, I knew extraordinarily little about my grandmother. She passed over twenty years ago, yet her most memorable warnings still ring in my head. "You can't tell everything you know" and "You better not tell what goes on under this roof." If I am The Vault, then she was Fort Knox.

We live in a tabloid culture in which no topic is off-limits. Celebrities and reality TV personalities disclose personal information to gain fame or remain relevant. Journalists, paparazzi, and trolls feel free to pose any question that comes to mind. Attention-starved, media-addicted civilians document every mundane routine on social media or comment rudely to people they have never met.

My greatest gifts in life are my friendships and the love of my small family. Their happiness and well-being are of the utmost importance to me. For me, consoling someone resembles sitting with him or her in a meditative silence or actively listening as they lament. I avoid treading into topics that have caused them pain or bombarding them with probing questions. If something unpleasant has happened to someone, they own the topic; it's theirs to bring up. Don't ask!

Some of my loved ones believe true intimacy and friendship requires complete vulnerability or being an open book. For me, it is having the knowledge, awareness, and patience to enable them to share their truths at their own pace. Though I operate under the assumption people will entrust me with their confidences in due time, I manage to convey my level of interest in their lives in other ways, such as sending "thinking of you" cards or meaningful gifts out of the blue.

* * *

Ms. Tina Fey is in the top five of my imaginary celebrity best friends, and it is my strong belief we were separated at birth. In her bestseller, *Bossypants*, she navigates the readers through occasions when people ask about the scar on her face, which was inflicted during a traumatic childhood attack by a stranger near her home. I am certain, as some of you are reading, there is an urge to know the intimate details of the attack. Yet if given the opportunity to meet her in person, most would not dare inquire. Ms. Fey deems those asking about the scar within one week of knowing her as "egomaniacs of average intelligence or less." [6] Please do not be an egomaniac of average intelligence and please don't allow your friends to be egomaniacs of average intelligence! Subjects such as Ms. Fey's trauma are just one of many landmine topics that should be avoided or broached with caution. Politics, religious convictions, and finances can be hot-button discussions among family and friends. Imagine the reactions with complete strangers.

Jennifer is one of my dearest friends and one of the most warmhearted people to ever come into my life. She recently informed us that she is on probation on Facebook. She explained she used profanity against a stranger who posted a vile message on her friend's page. Do you want to gander the subject of the original post? Politics.

Cool-headed Jennifer decided to "fight crazy with crazy." Friends on the group text gave her virtual high-fives and exclaimed he asked for it. Playing devil's advocate, I stated her friend can fight her own battles or address matters with "her" Facebook friends. Jennifer's response was the virtual eye roll.

Once relegated to conversations with acquaintances, news outlets have normalized political debates between

---

[6] Tina Fey, *Bossypants*, (Reagan Arthur Books/Little, Brown and Company, 2011), 11.

strangers, and social media is a platform for anyone to become a political pundit. To what end? Dinner party hosts purposely invite those with opposing views to dinner parties to spark lively conversations. I value when people speak their truth, even when it is uncomfortable for others to hear it. With that said, certain settings are not suitable for a debate or argument. Here is my advice:

1. Read the room. Is this the ideal audience for the topic? For example, if co-workers or business associates are in attendance, you may not want to divulge personal or political information. Ask yourself the question, "Would I have the same conversation and tone in front of my church family as I would with my fraternity brothers?" If your answer is yes, please reach out to me immediately for my 1-on-1 services.

   Is the crowd in a festive mood? If yes, then the likelihood they want to listen to complaints about achy body parts or a recent breakup are very slim.

2. Understand the consequences of the group knowing your views, especially when strangers are present. Expressing your disdain for something or someone could come back to bite you. For example, saying you do not like working with people from the East Coast may not bode well if someone in the group is from the area and could have potentially been a great customer or employer. Take heed.

Expressing prejudice or disparaging views is never acceptable. It is bad enough to hold despicable views but disseminating them is adding insult to injury.

Personally, my hot button questions surround marriage and children. For a period of time, I avoided visiting my small, hometown church because I grew weary of the mournful gazes from the elderly women of the congregation as they asked, "Nicky, you haven't found somebody yet?" As soon as I answer "no," I am peppered with a series of questions such as "Your doctor friends don't have anyone they can introduce you to?" These sweet old ladies want MY PLAN!

First, let me note that these gracious and loving women believe that I am a great catch and cannot fathom why someone has not snatched me off the market. I recognize they mean well and want to see me happy, yet I always wonder what response do they expect? I could offer, "My therapist prefers that I don't get married until I resolve all of my issues" or "Monogamy is not my thing." As an etiquette professional, those snarky comments can never slip from my lips.

More questions that tempt the devil on my shoulder are in regard to my appearance. "Nicky, you have gained so much weight." "Nicky, you've lost too much weight and look sick." "I love your hair. Is it real?" I have a close friend who, no sooner than I enter a room, sizes me up and says, "Is that Rent the Runway?" I throw her a "nicesty" glance and continue greeting the room. I have no shame renting designer apparel and, at times, have shared this information on social media. My issue is, why does she need to know, and why would she bring it up in that manner? A true compliment should not be followed by a request to quell curiosity. If someone has a generous spirit, they can provide additional details. Don't ask, and if asked, don't tell.

* * *

You could fill a book with lists of questions that should not be asked. No matter how proactive you are about putting up walls around specific subjects, there will always be inconsiderate people who overstep boundaries. Keep in mind, if you believe someone totally crossed the line, it is your right to firmly explain the query is inappropriate or disrespectful. The location does not excuse the intrusive query, but it can affect how you choose to respond. You need to decide if the behavior warrants a public or private response. Later in the chapter, the need for an intervention or escalation is discussed.

The next few pages will highlight various questions that can be perceived as invasive, explanations and implications from the questions, and tips from my toolkit for gracefully addressing these thoughtless or prying questions. Armed with these techniques, you will remain as unflappable as a Queen's Guard when dealing with "egomaniacs of average intelligence."

1. Redirection or Deflection
2. Question with a question
3. Humor
4. Silence and stares (i.e., dramatic pause)

WHY ARE YOU SINGLE?
WHY DID YOU NEVER GET MARRIED?

REDIRECT/ DEFLECT	ANSWER WITH A QUESTION	HUMOR
LET ME THINK ABOUT THAT OVERNIGHT.	I DON'T KNOW. WHY ARE YOU STILL MARRIED?	IDRIS IS ALREADY TAKEN!
MY TRAVEL IS THE ONLY THING I WANT TO BE MARRIED TO.	WHY DON'T WE TALK ABOUT MY RECENT PROMOTION?	I WAS. THANKS FOR BRINGING UP THAT PAINFUL PERIOD.
I'M MARRIED TO MY PURPOSE. LET ME TELL YOU MORE ABOUT IT.	DO I NEED TO BE MARRIED TO SPORT A FABULOUS RING?	I FORGOT TO UPDATE MY CREDIT CARD ON MATCH.COM.

Why is this question impolite and/or intrusive?

This question assumes that the goal, especially for women, is marriage. For those who have not been married, the assumption is something must be wrong with you. Single people should not have to justify their status.

After a long flight, I was hit on by a guy on the train from the airport. After discovering I had no aspirations for marriage, he asked, "Then who are you going to leave your belongings to?" Yes, he went there! His first mistake was not picking up on the physical cues that I was too exhausted to engage in a robust conversation. Then he proceeded without pause or awareness that his questions were rude.

There are dozens of scholarly studies on the "marital status bias" in the workplace and the healthcare system. That is why I recommend don't ask and don't tell to minimize potential discrimination.

Society's expectation of marriage also has a clock. As I browse my *People* magazine, I see the phrase "Married *at last*." Shortly before typing this, I was reading the Facebook responses for a recently wed former colleague. Mingled in between the customary congratulations are notes saying, "It's about time," rudely insinuating they had him on a timeline. I have noticed these backhanded well-wishes are typically reserved for those marrying over the age of thirty-five or in long-term relationships.

This glorious, never-married spinster is here to say, "Don't ask, don't tell!"

WHY DID YOU GET DIVORCED?
WHY DID YOU BREAK-UP?

REDIRECT/ DEFLECT	ANSWER WITH A QUESTION	HUMOR
THAT IS OLD NEWS. LET ME TELL YOU ABOUT MY NEW LIFE CHAPTER.	CAN YOU REPEAT THE QUESTION?	BEING THE THIRD SISTER-WIFE WAS NOT GLAMOROUS.
WE MAKE BETTER FRIENDS AND CO-PARENTS THAN SPOUSES.	YOU DON'T EXPECT ME TO GOSSIP ABOUT THE FATHER OF MY CHILDREN?	I LIKE FOLLOWING TRENDS AND DIVORCE IS THE NEW BLACK.
THAT SUBJECT IS TOO COMPLEX TO UNPACK OVER DINNER.	HOW DID YOU HEAR ABOUT MY DIVORCE?	I THOUGHT, WHAT WOULD JLO DO?

Why is this impolite and/or intrusive?

For some, divorce is a welcome state, and for others, it is an emotionally painful subject. If you have to ask, you probably are not as close to that person to feel entitled to a response. If a friend is recently divorced, politely ask if they need anything, send flowers, or offer to take them out for drinks.

WHY DID YOU NEVER HAVE KIDS?
DO YOU WANT CHILDREN?

REDIRECT/ DEFLECT	ANSWER WITH A QUESTION	HUMOR
SPEAKING OF KIDS, TRACY NAMED ME GODMOTHER TO HER BABY.	WHY DO YOU ASK?	I CANNOT GIVE UP CHAMPAGNE.
I AM HELPING CHILDREN VIA MY GIVING CIRCLE. LET ME EXPLAIN.	WHY DID YOU HAVE CHILDREN?	MY FUR BABY IS THE JEALOUS TYPE.
MY LIFE IS BUSY AND FULL AS IS.	ARE YOU TRYING TO GIVE AWAY ONE OF YOUR PRECIOUS ANGELS?	THERE NEEDS TO BE A CURE FOR STRETCH MARKS FIRST.

Why is this impolite and/or intrusive?

The topic of children is a way for some people to identify commonalities. However, you may not be aware of fertility issues someone may have faced or a child they may have lost. Bringing up this subject can be an emotional trigger. In addition, similar to the marriage question, it implies parenthood is the goal.

HOW OLD ARE YOU?

REDIRECT/ DEFLECT	ANSWER WITH A QUESTION	HUMOR
A LADY NEVER TELLS.	HOW OLD DO I LOOK?	ARE WE CARDING PEOPLE AT WORK NOW!
THAT IS NOT INFO THAT I WISH TO SHARE.	WHAT IS YOUR AGE?	DO YOU WANT MY MOTHER'S MAIDEN NAME TOO?
AGE IS A STATE OF MIND.	WHY DO YOU NEED TO KNOW?	I LOST TRACK TWENTY YEARS AGO.

Why is this impolite and/or intrusive?

On dating apps or at a bar, this question might be appropriate; however, in a business setting, it is not acceptable. There are conscious and unconscious biases based on age in the workplace and beyond. Society has expectations on what you should accomplish at specific stages. If you do not fit into this mold, then opinions might be formed that might be a detriment to you.

Here is an example of the type of assumptions that

are made in the business world. At a compliance conference, someone stated they would not hire a woman for a position that requires travel if she was visibly pregnant at the time of the interview. The interviewer is making assumptions about her life. Her husband could be a stay-at-home dad, or they may have live-in childcare. As long as they are qualified and attest to being able to perform all the functions of the job, then don't ask, don't tell.

ARE YOU WEARING A WIG? IS YOUR HAIR REAL? CAN I TOUCH YOUR HAIR?

REDIRECT/ DEFLECT	ANSWER WITH A QUESTION	HUMOR
THANKS FOR NOTICING MY NEW STYLE.	WOULD YOU ASK AN ELDERLY MAN IF HE IS WEARING A TOUPEE?	ALL QUEENS WEAR CROWNS!
EVERYTHING ON ME IS MINE.	WHO ELSE'S HAIR HAVE YOU ASKED TO TOUCH?	THIS IS JUST ANOTHER WITNESS PROTECTION DISGUISE.
HANDSHAKES AND HUGS ARE WHERE I DRAW THE LINE.	WHAT WOULD YOU ACCOMPLISH KNOWING THIS INFO?	SORRY, THE PETTING ZOO IS CLOSED.

Why is this impolite and/or intrusive?

Wearing wigs or weaves is not as taboo as it was twenty years ago. Though, as I said above, would you ask an elderly gentleman if he has a toupee? Or would you ask the co-worker across from you, "Are you a real blonde"? I hope your response was "no." Keep in mind, some people wear wigs due to medical conditions such as cancer and alopecia. Provide a compliment and keep it moving. If they want to divulge their beauty secret, so be it. Note: Touching someone or their hair as if they are part of a petting zoo is never acceptable.

Media mogul Oprah Winfrey speaks freely nowadays about her use of wigs. Speaking to Rob Lowe on his podcast, Oprah described a question she asked earlier in her career that still makes her cringe. When interviewing actress Sally Fields, she asked, "Does Burt sleep with his toupee on?" Though Sally was not involved with Burt Reynolds at the time, this was an extremely invasive and inappropriate question. Recognizing the inquiry was more for shock value, Sally immediately went cold and shut down. Reminiscing, Oprah learned from this experience and said she would not ask a similar question now.

DID YOU HAVE SURGERY?
DID YOU HAVE WORK DONE?
ARE THOSE REAL?

REDIRECT/ DEFLECT	ANSWER WITH A QUESTION	HUMOR
I KNOW YOU DID NOT MEAN FOR IT TO BE, YET I FIND THAT QUESTION INTRUSIVE.	ARE WE CLOSE ENOUGH TO DISCUSS THIS SUBJECT?	DO DENTAL IMPLANTS COUNT?
LET'S TAKE DISCUSSIONS ABOUT MY HEALTH OFF THE TABLE.	DID YOU FEEL I NEEDED SURGERY?	MY NEW SKINCARE REGIMEN WORKS WONDERS.
SURGERY IS SUCH A MACABRE TABLE TOPIC.	WHY DO YOU ASK? ARE YOU TRYING TO HAVE WORK DONE?	I WOKE UP LIKE THIS!

Why is this impolite and/or intrusive?

Questions regarding health and medical procedures are extremely personal, private, and, in some instances, legally protected. It would appear tabloid journalists asking these questions of celebrities have given everyone license to do the same. I would ignore this question or tell someone, flat out, it is inappropriate. In the work environment, it is best to steer clear of medical conversations completely.

Recently a friend disappointed me when recounting a tale of trying to determine if a woman had work done by giving insincere compliments and even asking to touch her body. This behavior is juvenile, mean spirited, and dangerous because it can be construed as sexual harassment. Your curiosity should not be quenched.

HOW MUCH DO YOU MAKE?

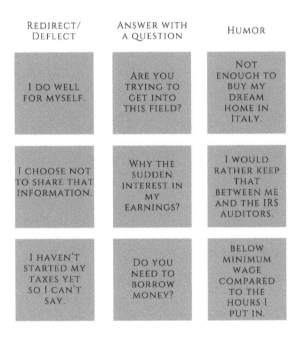

REDIRECT/ DEFLECT	ANSWER WITH A QUESTION	HUMOR
I DO WELL FOR MYSELF.	ARE YOU TRYING TO GET INTO THIS FIELD?	NOT ENOUGH TO BUY MY DREAM HOME IN ITALY.
I CHOOSE NOT TO SHARE THAT INFORMATION.	WHY THE SUDDEN INTEREST IN MY EARNINGS?	I WOULD RATHER KEEP THAT BETWEEN ME AND THE IRS AUDITORS.
I HAVEN'T STARTED MY TAXES YET SO I CAN'T SAY.	DO YOU NEED TO BORROW MONEY?	BELOW MINIMUM WAGE COMPARED TO THE HOURS I PUT IN.

Why is this impolite and/or intrusive?

The gender and racial wage gaps are real, yet discussing salaries, especially with your coworkers, can be a landmine. I have friends on both sides of the argument on whether to share wage information. One friend asks, "How do you know if you are leaving money on the table?" while another friend laments about the friction caused by her direct reports discussing this subject among each other.

While I empathize with both scenarios, I advise inquiring with Human Resources how they benchmark salary and where you fall or perform your own research online.

HOW MUCH DOES THAT COST?

REDIRECT/ DEFLECT	ANSWER WITH A QUESTION	HUMOR
IT WAS A GIFT.	ARE YOU IN THE MARKET FOR SOMETHING SIMILAR?	I DON'T LOOK AT TAGS OR RECEIPTS.
THIS OLD THING? I DON'T RECALL.	WORRIED I WILL NEED TO LIVE OFF YOU?	I ACTUALLY SHOPLIFTED THIS.
I BORROWED THIS FROM A FRIEND.	WHY ARE YOU ALWAYS IN MY POCKETS? (INSERT GIGGLE)	SILLY, IT WAS A PRESENT FROM YOU, DO YOU NOT REMEMBER?

Why is this impolite and intrusive?

This question is a backhanded method to find out how much you make, how you spend your money, or jealousy. An NYC-based friend is a single, Black fashionista. A fellow partner at her law firm inquiries about the price or designer of her clothes and has, on multiple occasions, looked at the labels of her jackets hanging on the door. In this setting, it is difficult to say, "mind your business," so the blank stare may come in handy. However, trip them up and ask "Are you a fashionista or trying to get a job on *Fashion Police* because you have a healthy preoccupation with my attire? Why is that because I find it a bit odd?" Another response could be, I have an aversion to people touching my clothes without washing their hands first.

DID YOU HEAR THE JUICY GOSSIP ABOUT...?

REDIRECT/ DEFLECT	ANSWER WITH A QUESTION	HUMOR
I BELIEVED YOU TO BE TOO EVOLVED TO SPEND TIME ON SALACIOUS GOSSIP.	HOW WOULD YOU FEEL IF YOUR LOVED ONE WAS THE TOPIC OF THIS STORY?	I HAVE NOT AND I WILL CHECK LATER TO SEE IF IT MADE IT TO INSTAGRAM.
MY LIFE IS SO FULL I DON'T HAVE THE DESIRE TO BE IN OTHER PEOPLE'S BUSINESS.	NOT YET, BUT WHAT JUICY GOSSIP DO YOU HAVE TO SHARE ABOUT YOURSELF?	I ONLY WANT TO HEAR IF IT IS ABOUT HER HITTING THE LOTTERY AND SHARING WITH US.
NO, AND I DO NOT MIND WAITING TO HEAR THE NEWS FROM THEM.	NO, DO WE NEED TO SEND HER FLOWERS OR A CARD AS A PICK-ME-UP?	WENDY WILLIAMS NEEDS TO WATCH OUT FOR YOU!

Why is this impolite and intrusive to you?

We all gossip. I will not engage in malicious topics or use someone's pain as entertainment. The serial, malicious gossipers are the ones you have to be prepared to shut down or steer onto more positive topics.

WHAT ARE YOU?

REDIRECT/ DEFLECT	ANSWER WITH A QUESTION	HUMOR
I AM A LOT OF THINGS. LET ME TELL YOU ABOUT MY CHARITABLE SIDE.	I'M AN ETIQUETTE EXPERT. DO YOU REQUIRE MY SERVICES?	I'M PART FOODIE, PART ROAD WARRIOR, PART FASHIONISTA.
I AM HUNGRY AND BUSY. LET'S QUICKLY ORDER SOME FOOD.	I'M A GIRL FROM CINCINNATI. DO YOU KNOW HOW TO SPELL THAT?	I'M A UNICORN.
I'M A DIEHARD CHICAGOAN.	WHAT DO YOU THINK I AM?	I'M EVERY WOMAN! (IN A WHITNEY OR CHAKA TONE)

Why is this impolite and intrusive to you?

Growing up, I never encountered this question because both my parents are Black, and everyone in my neighborhood and school knew all of us. As a "high yellow" Black woman, I may appear racially ambiguous, and people who do not know my background find that intriguing. Instead of bluntly asking the question, "What are you?", get to know the person and learn more about their history and heritage.

* * *

Everyone asks inappropriate questions at several points in their lives intentionally and unintentionally. Apologize, learn, and grow. I want to reiterate that you are not entitled to anyone's private or sensitive information, and you are not obligated to share or respond to questions you believe are invasive. The last weapon in my arsenal is the sideways stare. It is not an angry expression. It is a cross between confusion, inquisitiveness, and annoyance.

Now, it is your turn to practice. What reoccurring, pesky questions are you asked? Create your own nine box grid.

Don't Kill My Vibe

"Whining is just unbecoming."
–Dr. Maya Angelou

"Can we just all get along?" Heaven's no! Having an air of enlightenment is easy when people are nice, yet it is difficult to assume positive intent when people's words or behavior get under our skin. Some recognize our triggers and manage to pull them every opportunity they get. I advise not to take everything personally because wounded people lashing out is more about them than you. We cannot like everyone and not everyone will be a fan of ours. So how can we manage to co-exist with those intent on killing our vibe?

Vibe killers can come in many forms and have different tactics. There are the "death by a thousand cuts" in-laws, the proverbial nosy neighbor, the cantankerous uncle, the "elephant in a China shop" best friend, the "woe is me" sibling, the "attention- seeking, know-it-all" classmate, and of course, the person who calls the authorities when no offense is being committed. An entire chapter can be dedicated to ultimate Vibe Killers: mothers-in-law. I have firsthand accounts of these behaviors.

- A friend's husband told her his mom asked, "Why is she so skinny?"

- As a bridesmaid, I witnessed a mother-in-law wear dark shades throughout the indoor ceremony and reception.

- A married friend says her mom has photos of her high school boyfriends prominently displayed.

My recommendation would be to let your spouse know how you feel and have them hash it out with their parent. Let's not dwell very long discussing mothers-in-law. There are other frequent offenders.

DEBBIE & NELLY

Isn't it great to have people to commiserate with or just lend an ear? We laugh, cry, drink, repeat. With that said, I want to explain that friends are not dumping grounds or landfills for all of your issues. That is why you pay your therapist. With that said, I am not referring to those with depression or anxiety disorder, though these conditions can be an attributing factor. Debbie Downers or Negative Nellies are chronic complainers, glass half-empty people, who rarely have anything good to say, and find the negative in every occasion.

The worst part is these Gloom McDooms have the uncanny ability to spread their rain clouds and suck the joy from any room they enter. I asked a lady who works at my gym how she was doing, and her response was, "I woke up so mad." I said, "Then you should have gone back to sleep," then strolled to the next piece of equipment. At six in the morning, I could not follow her down that road.

It is not just their words that can alter the mood of a space. Sometimes it is their lack of speech, facial expressions, and body language that alter the mood. Allow me to share a real-life Debbie Downer in action and how I respond to them.

* * *

I love my Aunt Ruth. She is the elder stateswoman for what remains of our family. She is kind-spirited, supportive, and devout. In her late eighties, she lives independently and has overcome a bout of bone cancer. A conversation never ends before she tells me how proud she is of me and how my grandmother would feel the same if she was alive.

With that said, I must set hard stops to our calls because she will bring up every negative thing happening in the world today. Here are some examples of our talks:

"Aunt Ruth, how are you?"

"I am good, Nicky. How are you doing with all of

those killings in Chicago?"

"I'm alive, so it hasn't impacted me. How is Ms. Alice?"

"She has been having so many health issues."

"I'm sorry to hear that. She is truly blessed, though, to be living independently in her nineties. And thank God she has you as her neighbor. Tell her I said hello."

"Nicky, are you at home?"

"No, ma'am, I am out of town for work."

"You be careful. I saw on the news an airplane crashed."

"Having been in several car accidents, air travel is actually safer."

"Well, watch out for strangers. I heard about the killing and kidnapping of people overseas."

"I will make sure I pay attention to my surroundings no matter where I am. Just keep me in your prayers."

She will make every attempt to steer me into a world tragedy. Even after a four-hour nap on her couch due to the high heat and *Bonanza* re-runs, she will pick up right where she left off.

In these situations, take control of the conversation while remaining respectful and polite. Never attempt to provide solutions to problems. Humor or fact-checking are effective deflecting shields.

"Nicky, I can't believe how horrible Black people

dress these days. These young men walking around with their pants falling down their behinds."

"Aunt Ruth, where are you going to see such men?"

"I saw them on TV."

I laugh.

"Did you hear about a show called *How to Get Away with Murder*?"

"Yes, ma'am."

"I can't believe someone would make such a show telling people how to get away with murder."

"You know it is written by a Black woman?"

"I know! That does not make it right! Then you have all these men and women on TV doing whatever they want to do."

At this point, I shake my head and laugh as my friend explains the premise of the show to her. When I call or stop by to check on her, I make sure I have a legitimate out. On this occasion, Margo is my out. We have legitimate dinner plans. When I return to drop off food, Margo stays in the car, so I cannot stay for long.

My out again.

MARTYRS

At first glance, those with martyr syndrome seem like Good Samaritans, yet you eventually realize they are narcissists wanting attention and control versus genuinely wanting to help. I suspect most "martyrs" do not recognize this trait within themselves. They are overbearing, extremely judgmental, and bully their way to the middle of crisis under the guise of concern. They pat themselves on the back and often recount the many times they rescued friends from various situations.

As discussed in Don't Ask, Don't Tell, these are the people broaching sore subjects in your life. Due to their lack of awareness, they do not recognize the subject makes you uncomfortable. They want to pry their way into the situation, fight battles you have moved on from, hold grudges on your behalf.... I admit, at times, they get me worked up, and I join the fray.

You might not be able to avoid them because they may be co-workers or relatives. These individuals can be draining and combative; therefore, a game plan is needed when interacting with them. To disarm a person with this personality trait, I recommend:

1. Not divulging major problems to them,

2. Not asking for or accepting assistance from them, and

3. Showing minimal interest in their tales of saving damsels in distress or solving world hunger.

Otherwise, you are feeding their ego and limelight complex. When asked about personal challenges, explain to them that you have everything under control or someone else is taking care of the matter, then leave it at that. They might pry for details in an effort to pounce on even a small morsel of the action. Eventually they will bore of you because of your lack of attention to their harrowing tales or the lack of drama in your life. Don't let them kill you or your vibe.

APATHETIC ARNIES

Being a parent or caregiver is the hardest job in the world. Having the responsibility for the well-being of another life is tremendous. I chose not to be a biological mother, yet my much younger brother, nephews, and godchildren are a constant worry for me. I have had amazing teachers and adopted mothers who never had biological children yet impacted my life in immeasurable ways. Though I am not an expert in bringing up children, I can add value when it pertains to them in social settings.

Raise your hand if you have been in the movie theater, a wedding, or upscale restaurant with a crying child and the guardian is either immune to the noise or simply refuses to take the child out? Infants on planes are excluded from this conversation, though an irate toddler on a thirteen-hour flight from Dubai almost had me reaching for the emergency exit.

I truly empathize with parents needing a break. However, if the child is not happy, then no one is happy. A considerate individual would be mindful of disrupting the experience of other guests. Parents should recognize when a location is not appropriate for children. Years back, I went to see a holiday performance at Madison Square Garden with a co-worker. Our seats were up in the nosebleed section, but we still had an amazing view. A young mom sitting in front of us arrived late and continually struggled with her crying toddler throughout the show. Her apologies seemed sincere as people in the area got up to leave, but most confusingly she never removed herself from the equation.

How can situations like this be addressed? The polite approach would be to discreetly say, "I can watch your belongings or save your seat if you need to take the child out for a bit." Hopefully, they will get the hint. If that does not work, a direct method can still be respectful. Briefly explain you are having issues enjoying the performance and ask if they mind taking their adorable child out for a little bit. Now, if all fails, contact a member of the staff to address the situation by either moving you or them.

FOOD FOR THOUGHT

IN 2014, PARENTS BROUGHT AN INFANT, WHO BEGAN CRYING, TO A THREE-STAR MICHELIN RESTAURANT.

HOW SHOULD THIS SITUATION HAVE BEEN HANDLED?

GOSSIP FOLKS

During my tenure at the headquarters of a large cereal company, I vividly remember a portrait of a lone corn flake with the caption, "A Reputation is a Fragile Thing." Raise your hand if you have never gossiped. We all have been intrigued by tales from the rumor mill and likely will continue to be, especially about celebrities and politicians. I draw the line at mean-spirited, salacious gossip. This is when you get the sense that the bearer of the information is reveling in other's misfortunes or irresponsibly sharing privileged information. This person is a bonafide gossipmonger aka amateur Wendy Williams.

If you do not wish to be party to the gossip fest, politely excuse yourself or use some of the tools from the Don't Ask, Don't Tell chapter. Remember if they are being loose lipped about someone else, they are likely doing the same about you. Don't let them kill your vibe.

SPOTLIGHT

Tactless behavior, such as putting someone on the spot or deliberately embarrassing them in front of a crowd, is not appropriate, even though, in some cases, intentions were good. Typically, I witness this behavior when attempts are made to bring a shy person out of their shell. All it truly does is breed resentment from the recipient of such treatment and causes them to retreat further. I have lost count of the times I have cringed when someone believes asking questions or making a request in front of an audience will garner their desired outcome. Don't kill someone's vibe by putting them on the spot. If you are put on the spot, reply with a confused, sideways stare, accompanied by complete silence. Hopefully, this gives them time to correct their error.

CELL PHONES

The topic of mobile device etiquette could fill an entire book, and there is a chapter on "Netiquette" farther in the book. During a recent meditation class, the woman on my right snored through most of the experience. Then, when she awoke, she began searching the Internet on her phone. In the darkened space, the glare from a phone was quite distracting. During concerts, I have been behind people recording the entire time, and my eyes cannot help but to continue to glance at their screen. Now, are they really going to watch it again later, and are they truly enjoying themselves?

There are friends I do not enjoy going to any theater with. Though they attempt to shield their phone during performances, in my peripheral vision, it is like Times Square. My impolite alter ego wants to say, "Why do you think you are so important that you have to constantly check your phone?" When nudging or the "death eye" does not work, I threaten to move seats and that typically makes them put their phones away.

One of best events I attended in recent memory was a Dave Chappelle stand-up performance at a location that required all phones to be locked in a tamper proof sack. Also, add Miraval Spa in Tuscan, Arizona, to the list. This destination spa has an "unplug and be present" policy, and they even provide sacks and beds for your phones.

If you are the type who is constantly tempted to look at your phone, power it all the way down and practice only checking it during intermission.

The use of the speaker function in public or in the presence of others not participating on the call is disruptive and disrespectful. Invest in good headphones or excuse yourself. It is bad enough everyone must listen to your end of the conversation.

I have been on airplanes, in vans, and in close

quarters with people on speakerphones, and I wonder how they think this is okay. You can remedy this passive aggressively by making a call and placing your phone on speaker to compete with their conversation. Or slip them a note asking, "Do you need to borrow headphones?" or "Do you need me to take a quick break so you can have the privacy of the room to complete your call?" If you are close to the person, feel free to say, "Do you mind putting that away?"

Recently, at a wedding, I was delighted when the pastor stated the couple requested that guests refrain from taking photos during the ceremony. That is such an amazing idea. When I look at wedding videos or albums, all I see are the lights from cellphones ruining the ambiance of the moment. The couple paid good money for a photographer. Please let them do their job. Power down and don't kill the vibe!

YOUR HIGHNESS

Twenty years ago, I would not have imagined I would have to address "drug" etiquette! The legalization of recreational marijuana use has swept the United States. As of 2020, the state where I reside, Illinois, is one such state. I do not partake, nor pass judgment on those who do so legally. However, I have to wave my little, etiquette penalty flag (or napkin) pertaining to the use around others. Like cigarette smoke, I do not want the smell of marijuana trailing me or to have my hair and clothes reek of it. In addition, secondhand smoke may be a health hazard, so users should be mindful of this before lighting up around others.

Summertime in Chicago (#SummertimeCHI) is absolutely amazing. There are dozens of festivals around the city and activities on Lake Michigan. Prior to the legalization of marijuana use in Illinois, friends and I were laying on the grass (no pun intended) at a jazz festival when a couple next to us lit up. It was in a public park with children nearby. Since they lacked self-awareness, someone politely asked them to extinguish their joint, which they did. If they had not, a proper course of action would be to raise the issue to park security.

Here are my guidelines for marijuana use:

- Stay home and light up.

- Excuse yourself and light up in designated areas or graciously ask if others are comfortable with you smoking.

- Keep your butts to yourself and discard remnants in the proper, safe receptacle.

- Under no circumstances should you lace food with a substance and serve it to guests unknowingly.

- Remember, marijuana and other drug use may not be legal in the jurisdictions you are traveling to. Though I look quite nice in orange, I prefer not to get locked up because I am unknowingly with someone with a banned substance. Please and thank you!

PET-ETIQUETTE

I am the proud auntie to several fur babies and would go as far as to say I have joint custody of one adorable toy poodle. They bring me so much joy and lots of laughs. Yet I sadly realize that not everyone is a pet person.

Pet parents:

- Clean up after your babies!

- Do not ask people if it's okay if you bring your pet. More than likely, they want to say "no," yet don't.

- Remember some people are genuinely allergic to some animals.

- Call ahead to determine if restaurants, hotels, and stores are pet friendly.

- Do not permit your pet to jump up on people.

- Be mindful of your neighbors. If your baby experiences separation anxiety that results in constant barking, speak with your vet for options, before I slip them a CBD treat. Just kidding!

- Just like with children, pick them up and drop them off at the agreed upon time.

FUNERALS

For most, experiencing death is the most challenging time in a person's life. Whether it is a loved one, pet, or a favorite celebrity, managing your emotions during this period is difficult. This subject matter is not in this chapter with the belief death is a "vibe killer"; I intentionally placed it here based on behaviors exhibited. Grief and empathy for the grieving is not one size fits all. I have attended a spirited, jazz band fueled happy hour, in which the widow exclaimed this was the best funeral she had attended. Another was emotionally draining because someone was rushed to the hospital and died.

Typically, the mood is somber; therefore, here are some tips to respectfully pay your respects.

- Death is not a time for comparative suffering. Avoid turning the subject towards you. For example, if someone's parent died, do not start relaying your account about how you have a deceased parent.

- A person going through the grieving process is not looking for someone to "fix" anything. As a fixer, this is a challenge for me because I just want to make things right.

- It should go without saying that items, such as photos, should not be placed in the casket.

- Attire should be business or Sunday's Best solemn. Remember this occasion is about the deceased and the family.

- We live in a selfie society; however, the funeral is a private event and the loved ones of the deceased set the tone.

- The repast following the funeral is not meant to feed the multitude. If the turnout is large, take small portions to consume onsite to ensure the family has enough for all of their guests.

"Extreme Embalming"

The deceased is staged as if they are part of a Madame Tussaud's exhibit or enjoying activities they loved during their life (e.g., playing video games or poker, sitting at a bar).

Similarly, the Egyptians' burial practices focused on the afterlife based on what was needed during life.

* * *

VIBE KILLERS

ACTION	MY RESPONSE
SOMEONE PUTTING THEIR FEET UP ON MY TABLE OR DESK.	EXCUSE ME. I HAVE A NO SHOES ON THE TABLE RULE. CAN YOU GO GET A WIPE SO I CAN SANITIZE THIS AREA?
PEOPLE ENTERING A SPACE, THEN ADJUSTING LIGHTS, FAN, MUSIC, ETC. WITHOUT FIRST ADDRESSING IT WITH THOSE THERE BEFORE THEM.	DO YOU MIND TURNING THE LIGHTS OFF? WHEN I HAVE COMPLETED MY MEDITATION. I WILL TURN THEM ON FOR YOU ON MY WAY OUT.
UNDERHANDED COMPLIMENTS SUCH AS "YOU HAVE SUCH A PRETTY FACE," OR "YOU DO NOT SEEM LIKE YOU ARE FROM OHIO."	• THANKS! WHAT DO YOU THINK OF MY BODY? (INSERT GIGGLE) • HALLE BERRY AND LEBRON JAMES ARE FROM OHIO, SO I AM IN GREAT COMPANY!
FRIENDS WHO TELEPHONE ME YET HAVE FULL BLOWN SIDE CONVERSATIONS GOING ON (OR CALL SO I CAN LISTEN TO THEM BREATH).	THANKS FOR REACHING OUT! I SEE YOU HAVE A LOT COMPETING FOR YOUR ATTENTION. LET US CONNECT AT A LATER DATE.
MEN NOT INTRODUCING THEIR WIVES OR DATES.	WHO IS THIS LOVELY CREATURE ACCOMPANYING YOU?

Litterbugs, people not offering their seat to the elderly or expectant mothers, cars going slow in the fast speed lane, sidewalk hogs (the sea does not part for you), not wiping gym equipment after use, full-blown conversations while deplaning. Okay, I need to stop before you get the impression I have major issues!

What are your Vibe Killers? List them. That way, you have given them some thought and will be better prepared if and when they rear their pesky little heads.

Virtual Insanity

"Language is man's way of communicating with his fellow man, and it is language alone which separates him from the lower animals."
–Dr. Maya Angelou

A new British drama series follows a group of politicians as they manage a national crisis; the entire country loses power. Initially this spurred partying due to the belief the world was ending, yet within days, the country spirals into all out anarchy. Contemplate that, less than one-hundred years prior, electricity was not common in most homes worldwide. Lest you managed to find a way to live totally off the grid, being connected is ingrained in every aspect of our daily lives.

To paraphrase author Erik Qualman, it is not a matter on whether we use social media; it is a question of how well we use it. This is coming from a person whose foot instinctively jutted out to save her phone from hitting the ground. I can live with a bruised big toe but not without a cellphone. There is an ease to being connected. My next meal is just a few swipes away. Who needs to print out directions, carry credit cards, or wait on hold to schedule appointments? Not I! The playing field is leveling due to greater access to information and the ability organize with others across the globe. Charities and individuals can raise much-needed funds quickly. Communication barriers are broken down, and new languages are learned. Though the benefits are substantial, the Internet and electronic communication cause the most noise and conflict in the world.

Much gets lost in translation because tone is hard to detect online. For example, a woman responded to an NPR online article using sarcasm, which truly does not translate well online. By the end of the thread, she had been called a "meth head" and every other name but a child of God by people with whom she shared the same views. Some, upon recognizing their error apologized later in the comments, but what triggered them to respond so harshly (1) on a public forum and (2) to a person they never met. Not a day goes by that ordinary people lose their jobs or a celebrity is not walking back tweets or shuttering their social media accounts due to poor judgment and impulsive fingers. Bullying has morphed from school day antics to a vicious twenty-four-hour cyber-stalker. Trolls use their anonymity to spew hate-filled speech and operate unchecked. I am not professing that social media and the Internet turned individuals into oppressors and hecklers; it just expanded their reach.

* * *

Remember the good, old days when the opinions of strangers were private or our method of response, (e.g., calling, writing, paging), allowed time for cooler heads to prevail. As soon as children, and some adults, begin utilizing electronic devices, they need to be schooled on netiquette (internet etiquette). You do not have to be famous or high profile to have a multi-step communication and social media strategy.

Stage 1: Determine the medium

The art of polite conversation might be devolving due to technology. Choose how the topic is best addressed: mail, phone call, email, text, or face-to-face meeting. Here are the pros and cons of each.

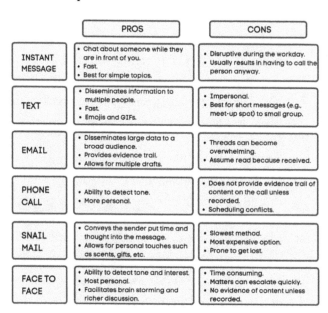

	PROS	CONS
INSTANT MESSAGE	• Chat about someone while they are in front of you. • Fast. • Best for simple topics.	• Disruptive during the workday. • Usually results in having to call the person anyway.
TEXT	• Disseminates information to multiple people. • Fast. • Emojis and GIFs.	• Impersonal. • Best for short messages (e.g., meet-up spot) to small group.
EMAIL	• Disseminates large data to a broad audience. • Provides evidence trail. • Allows for multiple drafts.	• Threads can become overwhelming. • Assume read because received.
PHONE CALL	• Ability to detect tone. • More personal.	• Does not provide evidence trail of content on the call unless recorded. • Scheduling conflicts.
SNAIL MAIL	• Conveys the sender put time and thought into the message. • Allows for personal touches such as scents, gifts, etc.	• Slowest method. • Most expensive option. • Prone to get lost.
FACE TO FACE	• Ability to detect tone and interest. • Most personal. • Facilitates brain storming and richer discussion.	• Time consuming. • Matters can escalate quickly. • No evidence of content unless recorded.

Stage 2: "Kill the Messenger!" Just kidding!

The phrase "don't shoot/kill the messenger" is meant to convey the messenger is innocent, though they may be the bearer of bad news. This does not hold true in today's world of social media. The messenger is not blameless and has great responsibilities.

1. Diamonds and the Internet are forever. Common sense worth repeating. Unlike *Mission Impossible*, messages will not self-destruct; they may explode. This goes for me, too. I pray for the day I am successful enough for someone to dig up dirt on me. Unfortunately, they may not have to delve too deep, so please allow me to pre-apologize.

2. For contentious topics, imagine you are addressing your grandmother, priest, or five-year-old child. Or pretend you will soon be announcing your candidacy for public office. This technique helps keep the focus on tone, the issue, and the resolution, versus pure emotion.

3. Social media should not be used to air grievances, breakups, or overshare. Plus, the messenger should not use all caps, because it infers yelling.

4. Emails, social media posts, and applications should all be saved in draft format before sending/posting. Walk away for a few minutes or a day, re-read, edit, then send.

5. Check the distribution lists, then re-check them. I would even go so far as to say stop using the Reply All function. Instead, take the time to enter each name individually. Despite what everyone says, they do not want to hear what is being said behind their backs unless it is good. Plus, privileged information could be disseminated to the wrong parties. I have been a witness, victim, and perpetrator in similar scenarios, and trust me, all are wretched.

6. Send one condensed email versus flooding mailboxes. This is especially true if the topics are the same.

7. Admittedly, one of my life goals is to have my autobiography created with just memes and GIFs. Though I use them relentlessly with close friends, I advise refraining from their use during official correspondence.

Stage 3: Know Your Audience

1. Avoid being social media friends with colleagues, business partners, and exes. If you are in marketing, then you may want to create two accounts if your work requires you to have a presence on social media.

2. Recognize that when you "like" a post the assumption is made you agree with the content. You are not giving a thumbs-up "just because."

3. Computer Love: Do not misrepresent yourself online, whether on a dating or a professional networking site.

Stage 4: Master Meetings

The importance of human interaction is critical for our emotional health. Though Zoom, FaceTime, and Skype were available before, the 2020 global pandemic has drastically changed the way we stay connected and do business. In lieu of funerals, virtual memorials have become popular. It goes without saying, many of the same rules apply for both online and in-person meetings. I would like to offer words of advice for flawless virtual meetings.

- Be on time. If you are the host, perform a test run, at least, one hour prior to the meeting to avoid technical difficulties.

- Dress appropriately for work calls. Business casual on top and bottom on the chance you have to stand up.

- Settings should be tidy or choose a simple virtual background.

- Actively listen, provide your undivided attention, and mute when not speaking.

- Minimize multitasking and moving around. Kids and pets are only cute the first time they disrupt a meeting.

- Do not take your phone with you for personal breaks (e.g., bathroom).

Stage 5: Profiling

Unless you are a professional Internet troll, your social media profile matters. In most cases, it is the first exposure potential employers or romantic partners have of you. Not only should your profiles be checked for grammatical errors, annually, an examination of bios should be performed to ensure they are in line with your current value proposition and personal brand.

The most noticeable element of any bio is the photo. First and foremost, the photo should be (1) recent and (2) it should be of you. That is a great start, and here are more checks to perform to ensure your profile shines.

My spirit animal is a cat. They are low-maintenance, regal, adaptable, and moody. Basically, the opposite of their needy canine counterparts, who I love as well. Since I do not want to embarrass anyone, what better way to demonstrate less than ideal business networking profiles than with my feline friends?

Express Yourself: Practice in the mirror. Though I am queen of the sideways stare, this, along with over-smiling, timid, and blank stares, should be avoided.

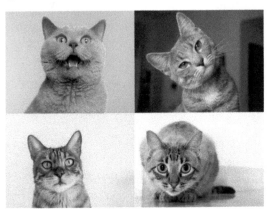

BAH HUMBUG: Unless you have a pass from Ms. Tyra Banks, please leave the "smizing" to professionals. There is a time and place for a stern face, and it is not your social networking profile.

No body shaming here, but they are called headshots for a reason. This definitely holds true for business networking sites. Ensure from the neck up is within frame and your full face can be seen.

Lighting and clarity are important. Ensure photos are not blurry or under-/over-exposed.

Reduce background noise. A tidy, crisp background is ideal to keep the focus on your fine face.

Having friends and loved ones is such a blessing. However, on business networking sites, you need to fly solo.

Artistic photography is great for social sites, but for professional and business pages, keep the poses basic.

Top cat. These pretty kitties got it right, though bookish cat is giving off a bit of attitude. The lighting is good, the full face can be seen, and the expressions are neutral.

Here are examples of headshots that are ideal. The images are clean, the lighting is perfect, the background is clutter-free, and the full face can be seen.

* * *

Additional guardrails your online strategy should include are:

- Minimize use at work and definitely do not access inappropriate sites, unless you are trying to get fired with cause.

- Allow parents to control their children's social media presence. Do not post photos of kids without the parents' permission.

- Don't post embarrassing photos of yourself or others.

- Check yourself into a location but leave me off. I might have told a fib that I was somewhere else.

- Stop oversharing. Don't make it easy for hackers or provide your company grounds to terminate you.

Your turn. Here is your magic wand. What would you change about social media and the Internet?

Work, Work, Work, Work, Work

"Nothing will work unless you do."
–Dr. Maya Angelou

I f someone asked me over thirty years ago where we would be as a society, I believed we would be operating flying cars like the Jetsons. Unfortunately, like flying cars, the vision of a cohesive society seems as far away today as it did when I was a child. No place is this more apparent than in the workplace. Work is where adults spend most of their waking hours in forced relationships and encounters with people who are most not like them.

Blatant discrimination is still alive and well, and according to the 2019 report *Being Black in Corporate America*[7], workplace prejudice often shows up in subtle ways known as "microaggressions," and Black professionals experience these microaggressions at significantly higher

---

[7] Hahna Yoon, "How To Respond To Microaggressions," The *New York Times*, March 3, 2020.

rates than all other racial groups they surveyed.[8]

Examples include:

- Colleagues have used racially insensitive language around me.

- Colleagues have touched my hair without my permission.

- I have been told I am "not like others" of my race/ethnicity.

- Others have characterized me as "angry."

After spending two decades in Corporate America, I have, unfortunately, been the witness and victim of several of these. I am not equipped to delve into the causes and solutions for microaggressions. What I can provide are techniques and suggestions on how to respond gracefully, yet firmly, when work confrontations arise.

- First promptly ask for clarity. I find that this often is a signal to the offending party that they may have crossed a line. "Excuse me, do you mind repeating that?" is a great example.

- Next, choose your battles wisely. Determine if this is a debate you want to press forward with

[8] *Being Black in Corporate America: An Intersectional Exploration*, Center for Talent Innovation, www.talentinnovation.org/_private/assets/BeingBlack-KeyFindings-CTI.pdf 2019.

by asking yourself:

- o How will this affect my working relationship with this person? If I do not respond, will I regret not saying something? If I do not respond, does that convey that I accept the behavior or statement?

If you decide to respond, determine if it is best served in private or in front of the audience in which the transgression occurred. Others may need the education as well.

- Explain why you find the comments offensive and how they made you feel. Feel free to add the opening: "I do not believe you intended to offend ..." to graciously give them an out. If they decide not to take the out, then that is a reflection of their bad manners and/or character.

- Document the event and, depending on the severity of the offense, raise it in writing to management.

WORKPLACE FAUX PAS

"Bring Your Whole Self to Work" is a recruitment and retention slogan for companies I cannot get behind. Code-switching, the act of altering how you express yourself based on your audience, is critical for Black Americans to survive and thrive in the workplace.

Politely, yet firmly, setting boundaries in the workplace is a necessity for Black Americans. Here's an example from a past work experience.

Coworker: "For Shizzle."

Me: Confused, direct stare. "Excuse me. I don't know what that means."

Coworker: "You don't know what 'for shizzle' means?

Me: "No." Of course, I knew the phrase made famous by Snoop Dogg, and she knew I likely knew. My confusion revolved around why she was saying it to me in a work conversation.

Coworker: Moment of clarity, casts her eyes down, and then moved on to other work topics.

If she would not use that kind of speech with the VP of the department, then she should not be using it with me. There was no need to raise my voice or get hostile to get my point across.

The stare, playing clueless, and tone was efficient and effective. A close friend, who is in her late-thirties yet looks much younger, is a Black vice-president at her company. She recounted a time when she was driving to a site with a young man who was new to the company, and she was his superior. He excitedly mentioned he wanted to turn on some music he believed she would enjoy.

After listening to a few profanity-laced verses of a rap song, she politely asked him to switch to another genre of music and left it at that. Many of us are thinking, how he could think that this music was appropriate to play in front of any coworkers, let alone his superior. Was this a teachable moment? Probably. It occurred so quickly; a well-composed counteracting response was not made. Upon reflection, she agreed this was a missed opportunity to educate him on why this was unacceptable.

BUSINESS ETHICS

Never over-drink alcohol or partake in drugs during work dinners or events, though others are taking it to excess. A polite response can be you have to drive, or you have an early morning.

This next recommendation is from a friend from work. During a working lunch, a new young coworker snacked from a bag of Andy Capp's Hot Fries, which are not a product manufactured by the food company for which they worked. My friend coached her to refrain from bringing in a competitor's snack.

Recently, I took the plunge of being an entrepreneur. Having consciously supported minority-owned businesses my entire life, here is some guidance from both sides of the coin.

BLACK BUSINESSES

In 2017, the Prosperity Now and the Institute for Policy Studies' *The Road to Zero Wealth* report indicated that the median wealth of Black Americans will fall to zero by 2053 if current trends continue. There are many historical and social factors contributing to this statistic, but from an etiquette perspective, here are situations we need to address.

- The "homey hook-up" can kill Black businesses. Buyers do not expect things for free. The polite alternative would be wait until the business owner offers a discount or barter your services.

- Address complaints privately with the business owners before escalating to social media.

- Respect others' time. Years of my life have been lost waiting at the salon. Raise your prices, hire an assistant, say "no," or better manage your calendar.

- Master customer service. If we are to succeed going forward, we must provide impeccable customer service. If you cannot hit a deliverable, be proactive and contact the customer. Do not wait for them to hunt you down. Stop over-promising and under-delivering. I am still waiting on a custom product I ordered from an

Instagram star. Each time I reach out, she has an excuse and even had the nerve to have an irritated tone. Of course, I will never order from her or recommend her business, no matter the quality of the product.

Guess Who's Coming To Dinner?

"And, no, it is not just about food. Food is very important because there are very few times we can be more intimate, as to share food together."
–Dr. Maya Angelou

A nother passion of mine is fine dining. Growing up, I barely recall a time when we ate outside our home or school. Do not get me wrong, both of my grandmothers were amazing home chefs, so we were truly fortunate. My Grandma Mary was especially masterful in the kitchen and on the grill. I still dream about her chili, chicken and egg noodles, stuffed green peppers, and bread pudding, which she made from frozen leftover toast. However, I never had the opportunity as a child to expand my palate to other cuisines.

THE FINER DINERS

Fortunately, work and pleasure afforded me the opportunity to travel the world for over two decades.

During these travels, I have become a fine-dining connoisseur. Those searching for a great meal reach out to me for recommendations, and my social media feeds are loaded with images of the most creative and delicious cuisines from around the world. Family and friends tease me for frequenting restaurants that serve "pretty food" or eating "rich people food."

The calls for recommendations and friendly teasing does not surprise me because I have witnessed, over the course of my culinary experiences, the lack of people who look like me. Not only the guests, but also among the staff and chefs. I recognize that, due to the price point, for those not on expense accounts, it is out of reach for most, unless for a special occasion. The question remains, why is there so little representation of Black Americans in the fine dining world, especially since we have a rich history in this space.

The film *The Butler* was inspired by Wil Haygood's *Washington Post* article "A Butler Well Served by This Election,"[9] where we are introduced to Eugene Allen, a Black man who served a thirty-four-year tenure in the White House as a butler. The film grants us access into the lives of the Black members of the service staff as they masterfully orchestrate their duties at elaborate state

---

[9] Wil Haygood, *A Butler Well Served By This Election*, The Washington Post (November 2008) https://www.washingtonpost.com/lifestyle/a-butler-well-served-by-this-election/2019/01/02/b2a805a6-07b1-11e9-88e3-989a3e456820_story.html

dinners and soirees, while being invisible and marginalized in society.

In the article "What It Was Really Like to Be a Black Butler in Mid-Century Washington," Daphne Muse writes about her father's and uncles' experiences as "Beltway Butlers." She eloquently states, "... it may be easy to imagine the Beltway Butlers as shuffling servants. But these men were consummate professionals, at times knowing more about protocol than those they served."[10]

The men of the Muse family were valued for their discretion, as well as their culinary capabilities. Many of these Black butlers had refined palates and were master carvers. Their jobs enabled them to expose their families to some of the most expensive and rare foods and spirits in the world.

Style and home icons such as my personal favorite, the late great B. Smith, brought formality, style, and grace to the dining experience on her TV programs and in her New York restaurant, which I visited on multiple occasions.

The National Museum of African American History and Culture in Washington, D.C. has a silver-plated tea service on display that was once owned by a prominent free Black family in Boston. In the 1850s, they lived in a fashionable neighborhood, and this tea service was used when they hosted abolitionist luminaries.

---

[10] Daphne Muse, *What It Was Really Like to Be a Black Butler in Mid-Century Washington*, The Atlantic (September 2013).

During the first half of the twentieth century, there were tea rooms started by and catering to Black Americans, cropping up across the United States. For example, Georgette's Tea Room in Miami, the Booker T. Washington Tea Room in Lexington, and the Ideal Tea Room in Chicago.

Why the history lessons, you ask? I want to demonstrate that Black Americans have historically been well-versed in fine dining and proper use of tableware throughout the history of this country. I am not suggesting the Western style of dining is best, but it is the genre I am versed in. Many non-Western societies throughout history have had strict hierarchical dining customs, which I respect and abide by when dining in these settings.

History and society have relegated Black Americans to be only masters and purveyors of informal styles known as Soul and Southern cuisines. The appreciation for culinary protocol, diversity, refinement, and curiosity has a place in the Black community, and it needs to be nurtured. I am going to do my part by championing and supporting diverse chefs and exposing the next generation of Black American foodies to the etiquette of fine dining.

Advice for all first-time fine diners:
- Do not be intimidated.

- Step out of your comfort zone.

- Ask questions. If you do not recognize an ingredient or preparation method, ask the server.

- Plan. Look at the menu and photos online prior to your meal.

- Send items back for quality issues (e.g., hair in food, under/over-cooked) not taste preferences.

- Taste food before requesting additional seasoning.

- Learn the tools of the table. Invest in a formal dining etiquette course for you and your entire family. If you have an important dinner on the horizon, and there is a time constraint, follow the lead of the host or take an online refresher course.

HOME DINING & ENTERTAINING

An etiquette mentor of mine is an amazing interior designer. Her impeccable taste and gentile manners set her apart from most. She has lived in Italy and Spain and traveled the globe.

Her philosophy on dining is at the heart of the opening quote from Dr. Angelou. Eating is more than the food.

Her home is a treasure memorializing a rich life lived across many cultures. What I love most are her chests of fine cutlery. An important lesson she taught me is to fine dine at home. When she was designing my apartment, she emphasized the need to discard tattered dishes and use the good china regularly.

Paper plates and plastic cups are a modern construct and, in my opinion, represent the disposable society that we live in. Every meal is special, therefore, break out the good china any day of the week. Let's bring the etiquette, art, and ceremony back to dining.

* * *

During my time at Macy's Corporate in the early 2000s, I sat in the office of a work friend as he mentioned he would be hosting a dinner party that upcoming weekend. At the end, I said, "Remember to make me a plate." His silence and blank stare made me register he had no clue what I was talking about. He asked if I meant ceramics, and I cried with laughter. Since his partner of many years was Black, I assumed he had been schooled in Black food traditions.

The following day, he exclaimed that he had been brought up to speed on what "making a plate" meant. In his family, they never thought of taking a serving of food to go. He described how, once, when he was visiting his parents, his mother packed a small container of a leftover item. But "the plate" is not leftovers—it is a smorgasbord of virtually all the food served.

Advice:

- Attention should be paid to people and polite conversation, not the food.

- Unless you are at the home of a family member or close friend, do not intend to make a plate. If offered, take small portions.

- If you are at the home of a relative or church event, please have a generous spirit and do not make a plate until every-one has arrived and been served. More people will have a chance to eat.

- Abstain from bringing additional guests unless you first confirm with the host.

- As a friend's grandmother proclaims, 'Don't come with two long arms." Bring a hostess gift (e.g., bottle of wine, chocolates) or a covered dish for potluck dinners.

- Whatever you bring stays. If the bottle you bring goes unopened, it remains. Plan to reclaim dishes you brought or transfer food to another container provided by the host.

- Refrain from complaining about the food. If you have a restrictive diet, inform the hostess at the time of accepting the invitation.

- At home, practice proper dining etiquette, at least, once a week. Always eat with the proper tools of the table.

- Remember to send a timely, handwritten thank you note to the host.

DINING OUT

There is no dining topic more contentious than splitting the check. It is a reason I avoid going to restaurants in big parties or fine dining with people I do not know. I have been the witness and victim of cringe-worthy incidents. Here are a few stories I received on the matter:

- A dinner where a guest did not chip in for the birthday girl and did not provide enough to cover her own check.

- During group dinners, someone always orders a to-go meal for their spouse yet expects the check to be split evenly between those attending the meal.

- A couple that dines with others but does not split the bill by person.

- A guy who vanishes when it is his turn to buy a round of drinks.

- People who do not tip. Unfortunately, Black Americans have a notorious reputation for being poor tippers.

Solutions:

- My friends and I typically split the bill evenly with the knowledge it all evens out eventually.

- If you are on a strict budget or with a group, then discreetly ask the server to split the checks prior to ordering. Or simply do not go.

- Another option is to arrive at the conclusion of dinner, order a drink, and chat with the remaining guests.

Bon Appétit!

Celebrate Good Times... Come On!

"I try to see every day as a celebration."
—Dr. Maya Angelou

Remember the good, old days when showers and birthday parties were intimate gatherings in someone's living room? Now they are full-blown Cirque du Soleil productions. Nuptials now include a death-defying public proposal, engagement parties, multiple bridal showers, and destination bachelorette/bachelor weekends with matching outfits for the Gram! Plus, the wedding party must learn choreographed dance routines to walk down the aisle and for the reception. I have not even mentioned the dresses, alterations, hair, make-up, and gifts.

According to a 2017 WeddingWire study, the cost of being a bridesmaid is about $1,200 to $1,800 per wedding. As a former finance professional, I believe this figure is extremely low.

Let us analyze it. A group of college friends are likely to have the same life stages. Several will get married within one to two years of each other, have kids around the same time, and have milestone birthdays in the same year.

Birthday celebrations and baby showers are just as all-consuming. There are birthday trips abroad and elaborate gender reveal parties. Joyous occasions should be celebrated! Yet pocketbooks and vacation days have limits.

We could barely keep up with the Joneses; now we are trying to keep up with the Kardashians. This is especially true of the younger generation, who has yet to build savings or emergency funds.

The pressure or guilt of not participating is overwhelming. I have been a witness to and victim of shaming. Accusations like, "I saw on Facebook you took a trip with that group of friends, but you have never done a trip with me" OR "You can afford a vacation, yet you can't contribute to the festivities."

We want our loved ones to feel special and shine on their big day, yet some of their demands may feel unreasonable or excessive. We begin equating friendship with the willingness to placate the star of the show, and we do not want to come across as jealous or stingy.

So how do we handle celebratory events with grace and avoid having it take a toll on the friendship and finances?

* * *

I DO... SORT OF

I adore weddings! The dresses, the flowers, the venues, the table displays . . . and, of course, the love of two people! I will not leave a reception until I have a slice (or two) of wedding cake. Sure, I can get cake anytime, anywhere, but there is something magical about wedding cake. What isn't there to love about weddings?

As a twenty-year plus veteran of the bridesmaids circuit and a professional guest/party crasher, I know a thing or two about weddings. One of the funniest scenes from *Sex and the City* occurs in a Vera Wang fitting room. Cinderella-esque bride-to-be Charlotte exclaims, "It's supposed to be my week," and Miranda shoots her a glare and says, "You get a day. Not a week." Note: Out of my friends, I am Miranda. Though I am not as harsh as Miranda, I do believe there should be boundaries and ground rules for everyone involved.

NOT SO FUN FACT

GENDER REVEAL PARTIES HAVES RESULTED IN DEATHS AND AN ARIZONA WILDFIRE THAT CAUSED $8 MILLION IN DAMAGES.

THE BRIDE AND GROOM

Typically, I am the one crying at the weddings of my close friends. Though I am not a hopeless romantic, I am overwhelmed by the love and joy from the ceremony. With that said, there are ways to make the journey down the aisle as smooth as possible for everyone.

Here are tips to be more gracious.

- It is rare for someone to turn down the request to be a part of the bridal party. When they provide their response, they are going in blind. The thoughtful course of action prior to "the ask" is having the location and estimate of the cost. One of my best friends told me she was phased out when she had to decline an overseas wedding.

- Do not ask someone, especially if they are not a relative or part of the bridal party, to throw you a shower or bachelorette party. People who want to do this will volunteer. Those who are asked to feel too uncomfortable to say "no" or don't want to embarrass you. Plus, if you do not have a shower, no one will miss those repetitive games.

- The dates of the wedding are likely tied to the availability of the venue. Having only fifty-two weekends to choose from, the celebration will likely conflict with other events. Be mindful of the dates if you want key people to attend... rethink proximity to holidays, births, other friends' weddings, etc.

- Do not take it personal if a friend or guest declines an invitation to your wedding. Just appreciate and focus on those who will be attending.

- Do not invite people to the showers and parties, and not invite them to the wedding and reception. This is extremely tacky and gives the appearance you are fishing for gifts.

- Start the wedding on time; otherwise, have an open bar and appetizers while guests wait.

- Allow people over thirty-five to opt out of the bouquet toss. Okay, this is not critical, just something I wanted to add.

THE BRIDAL PARTY

I love dressing up and going to weddings. Plus, I am dependable and not cheap. As a result, my bridesmaid resume was on the top of the pile during wedding season in my twenties and thirties. The Do's and Don'ts of wedding etiquette is my forte. In the following pages, I will share my expertise for the bridal party. If your finances are strained, or you believe the wedding expenditures are too extravagant, what do you say? Here are some sample responses to assist the flow of the conversation:

- 'I am honored you want me to be a part of your big day. Full disclosure, my savings are not where I need them to be, and I cannot incur more debt. Would you be offended if I had to opt out of some of the festivities?"

- 'I am super excited about being your bridesmaid. I need you to be aware the wife and I are saving for a house, so we are closely monitoring our expenditures."

- "Thank you for including me. I sincerely want to be a part of your big day. As you are aware, I'm between jobs. I do not want to disappoint you; however, I cannot afford this responsibility, and I do not feel comfortable borrowing money to cover my costs. How else can I help?"

- Do not volunteer to host or perform tasks you do not have the bandwidth for. Leverage the entire bridal party and parents to help with the logistics. Remember, it is not about you! Be supportive.

- Do not wait until the last minute to get things done, such as ordering the attire, alterations, and booking travel. Not doing this may cause undue stress on the couple.

- Order your garments timely and in the correct size. I am a witness and perpetrator of not choosing the correct size, believing the weight would magically dwindle. This causes unnecessary stress for everyone.

GUESTS

Guests have the easiest job at a wedding. Show up on time and help celebrate. There are two areas that guests may need some guidance.

Attire: Please pay close attention to the dress code, and if you make the decision to attend, please abide by it. Though you may not be a fan of formal dress or dislike when the host requests everyone wear the same color, you just have to power through it for a few hours.

Gift giving: Registries are the couple stating explicitly, "This is what we want," and not an opportunity for you to gift them what you want them to have. Stick to the registry or provide a monetary gift. Guidance for the value of the gift varies on your relationship with the couple, the estimated value of your meal at the reception, or foremost, what you can afford. Note: Sending the gift prior to the wedding saves you the hassle of lugging it to the venue.

RSVP: If you receive an invitation, respectfully reply in

advance of the due date for the couple to plan accordingly. If your plans change, contact the wedding coordinator or the couple and inquire if there is space. Remember, the invitation is typically just for you or a plus one! As they say, "No ring, no bring." Bringing random dates or plus ones should be avoided. Also note if the invitation states whether the occasion is for adults only.

BIRTHDAYS

My fortieth birthday party was a major bash at the Chicago House of Blues. That weekend is one of my most cherished memories, and my heart is still full because so many people braved a freezing Chicago winter to help celebrate.

A tropical birthday vacation is always welcomed since I have a January birthday and live in Chicago. The fact my birthday is two weeks after the wallet-draining Christmas holiday and vacation days are not accrued, I chose a party and covered the expenses. The task of organizing and deciding the invitees for a trip was extremely daunting.

Wouldn't it be ideal for groups of friends with a milestone birthday to combine their destination celebrations to minimize the costs for everyone? Since this is not likely to happen, here are some guidelines:

- Do not take offense if someone declines the invitation. Assume positive intent!

- Similar to weddings, have the maximum estimated expenses prior to "the ask." I specify maximum because, if the costs are dependent upon the number of people going, it could fluctuate if people drop out.

- Know thyself and know thy friends! If you want to have a gourmet-themed birthday party, then your meat and potato friends may pass. Do not feel obligated to address everyone's needs. You want what you want!

- Friends with children are passionate about birthday celebrations. In one instance, a friend's son was invited to a birthday party that had a strict headcount. She offered to pay for her daughter to attend; otherwise, she would have to find someone to watch her or arrange for her son to go with others. Parents may see value in stating "no gifts please" or donating to a cause and including the receipt in a card.

  Another friend explicitly requests no gifts for their son's birthday and to donate to a charity instead. Some people either (a) bring nothing (or no donation receipt) or (b) they bring him a gift, saying, "We don't think that's fair to him." Seriously, both of these examples happen every single year!

FRIENDS

If you cannot participate in the celebration(s), here are some sample responses to assist the flow of the conversation:

- "My PTO has already been used or accounted for. Let us do dinner or let me put some money towards your expenses for the trip."

- "I cannot make it to dinner because I will be fasting or on a strict diet during that time."

- "Let me buy you dinner later, or can I give you a gift certificate towards your meal?"

For situations arising in which you must cancel, notify your friend immediately and understand you may not receive a refund for deposits. Once you agree to attend, have a positive attitude, even though you are not aligned with the agenda or costs.

You should avoid questioning your friend's party plans and guest list. It's their celebration, not yours, so queries such as, "Who else did you invite to this party?" or "Why didn't you invite…" are inappropriate and center your needs above theirs.

I have to regretfully admit my friends and I are frequent offenders of this faux pas. Our motive for asking is to find out if there are any eligible bachelors we need to mingle with or, in the case of destination weddings, if there is someone we can split the room costs with. In the future, we need to ask questions specifically to our motives.

HOLIDAYS

In theory, holidays are the most joyous occasions, filled with good manners and cheers. Yet holidays, especially those occurring towards the end of the year, can be the most stressful times, emotionally and financially.

Growing up, we were not lavished with gifts or elaborate celebrations. Family stressors and commercialism have overshadowed the true sentiment of these holidays. Here is advice to help you survive the holidays unscathed.

POTLUCK CELEBRATIONS

- Create a sign-in with specific categories to have a diverse array of food and to avoid a commotion over who made the best dressing. Try SignUpGenius or Google Docs to electronically manage these details.

- If you sign up to bring a main dish, you need to arrive on time or drop off the dish, then return later. One year, I had a holiday party at my home, and the person responsible for the macaroni and cheese arrived well after everyone had eaten. I am still bitter about that one.

- If you are someone who tends to be the last to arrive at an event, offer to bring the dessert. However, if you are convinced the guests would be disappointed if they do not have your signature dish, prepare it the prior evening.

- I was blessed with having no food aversions. Back in the day, food allergies were never a cause for pause when at Black American functions. Pork was the only item people avoided. Always be prepared to inform the host or guests of the ingredients in your dish.

- Remember the rules in the chapter Guess Who's Coming for Dinner when making to-go plates.

- Return for your dish later or bring your contribution in a decorative, one-use container. Once the host has beautifully arranged the spread, do not interrupt the festivities in an attempt to get your dish back.

- Remember to send a timely thank you note, citing specific elements you enjoyed from the dinner.

- Be gracious and remember the spirit of the holidays.

Additional tips:

- Leave the crowds behind when you are a guest at a party, especially if you are not bringing provisions!

- When you walk into the room, allow the host to introduce you or introduce yourself to others if the host is unavailable.

- Hosts should provide party expectations at the time of the invites (e.g., costume). One of my dear friends informed me of his disco-themed brunch just a few days prior, and I had to cancel because it was not feasible for me to show up to a closely scheduled previous commitment looking like an extra from Saturday Night Fever.

- Provide the same gift to everyone. For example, donations to their favorite charities or gift cards.

- Do not use flash photography in small venues. WHY? It is distracting.

- The most frequently asked questions start with "Can you go..." or "Can you do...". Never feel obligated to respond affirmatively and, most importantly, do not feel the need to justify your response.

You Wear It Well

"The issues which face us all are not just how to survive, obviously, we are doing that somehow, but really how to thrive with some passion, some compassion, some humor and some style."
–Dr. Maya Angelou

"To dress within the formal limits and with an air gives men, as the Greek line testifies, authority." (Quintilian 100 - 35 AD); *"The apparel oft proclaims the man."* (Shakespeare 1609); *Clothes maketh the man.* "Clothes and manners do not make the man; but when he is made, they greatly improve his appearance." Proverbs throughout the ages about the impact of dress still ring true. Just recently, I watched a documentary on late style icon Audrey Hepburn, who surprisingly was self- conscious. She said what helped her the most throughout her Hollywood career were the clothes because they helped her look the part and provided confidence.

Let's get the obvious out the way. We all have judged a book by its cover. The assumptions made about someone's economic status, sexual orientation, or gender are based on the clothes they are wearing. Attire and appearance can convey religious beliefs, profession, affiliations, or circumstances. For example, if you see someone running down the street in an orange jumpsuit, your first thought would not be, That person is participating in a marathon.

While working in the Department of Finance in college, several of us were chatting about the recent wedding of a recent alum who previously worked in the office. For those who attended the wedding, the first question they were peppered with was, "What did the dress look like?" An eavesdropping professor commented that he believed women dress more to impress other women than for potential suitors. The jury is out on whether this is accurate, but our question demonstrates there is an innate focus on fashion.

Allow me to share a more recent example. While on a work trip, the young man working for me at the time arrived in the lobby wearing thong sandals. When our VP and director arrived in jeans and sports jackets, their eyes, like mine, swiftly locked onto the young man's toes. During work hours, his business casual appearance was perfectly fine, yet his wearing extremely casual sandals to dinner was a misstep. No pun intended. What if the VP decided we were going to an upscale restaurant with a strict dress code? My advice for him was maintain the same dress code the entire day if you are interacting with colleagues or suppliers after hours.

The admiring gaze of others or religious and professional requirements are not the only considerations when choosing which frock to don. How an article of clothing, shoes, hairstyle, or lipstick makes you feel is a determinant as well. What emotions or memories are triggered? Why do you dress a particular way? It is because you deem an occasion special or sacred. For example, most would not wear a jogging suit to a wedding, to meet the president, or to your parent's funeral. Celebrate every day and dress as such. Though I honor everyone's fashion choices, I am old-fashioned in this respect and am prepared for the respectability politics comments.

KEEP IT REAL
THE AUTHENTICALLY REFRESHING COUNTRY MUSIC STAR DOLLY PARTON ONCE QUIPPED, IT COSTS HER A LOT OF MONEY TO LOOK CHEAP. MS. PARTON IS AN ICONIC, LARGER THAN LIFE PERFORMER AND CELEBRITY.

FOR US MERE MORTALS THE LESS IS MORE APPROACH IS BETTER WHEN IT COMES TO WIGS OR EYELASHES, PLASTIC SURGERY OR INJECTABLES, FINGERNAILS AND CLOTHING. THIS ESPECIALLY RINGS TRUE IN THE WORK SETTING. IF FOLKS ARE BAFFLED BY WHETHER IT IS FAKE OR NOT MEANS YOU ARE ON THE RIGHT TRACK. KEEP THEM GUESSING!

Dressing casually has never been my forte, and I take great care curating my looks. While I am channeling a bohemian goddess, a no-nonsense businesswoman or a red-carpet diva is when I feel my best. Top it off with my signature bright lip and perfectly coiffed crown, and I am energized. What gives you that feeling? Wearing your favorite color, a fresh haircut and shave, new shoes?

* * *

My career started off at one of the world's largest fashion retailers, and I quickly learned how to shop effectively. Timeless, classic, well-made items never go out of style. The bygone era of wearing white gloves and dresses every day would have suited me fine. As mentioned earlier, my grandparents reared me; therefore, this influenced aspects of my style. As bone cancer withered my Aunt Ruth's size-fourteen frame, she bequeathed to me a box full of slips that I have to this day. I was taught, if a dress is not lined, a slip must be worn. Try finding a slip these days or inexpensive clothing with lining. Is there an unsaid classism of sheer clothing?

Elders in my family did not have large, glamorous wardrobes, yet they took great care of what they had while looking "casket sharp." My grandfather hand-shining his shoes are some of my most cherished childhood memories. His slim, long frame in freshly pressed, elegant suits was a sight to be seen. "Sunday's Best" was the measurement by which our attire was judged. Black-tie and cocktail attire was never spoken of because we rarely had occasions to dress in such garments. One Sunday morning, while in high school, I wore a pair of pantyhose so sheer my grandmother exclaimed, 'I know you ain't going to church bare-legged." Of course not! I recognize, *"Dressing well is a sign of good manners."* (Tom Ford).

Always err on the side of being overdressed or wearing something that can easily be converted from day to evening. What is considered professional or proper attire is subjective, yet we know there are unwritten rules, especially for people of color, which can impact us in social and business settings. Beauty and style shaped by Black culture is ubiquitous in mainstream fashion today, yet this does not prevent biases towards this population. Recent progress against prejudice, such as the 2020 California CROWN Act, prohibits discrimination based on hairstyle and hair texture.

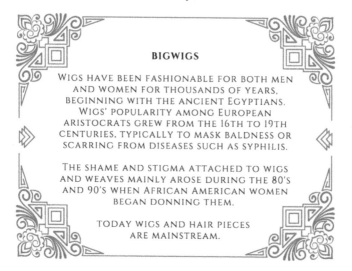

BIGWIGS

WIGS HAVE BEEN FASHIONABLE FOR BOTH MEN AND WOMEN FOR THOUSANDS OF YEARS, BEGINNING WITH THE ANCIENT EGYPTIANS. WIGS' POPULARITY AMONG EUROPEAN ARISTOCRATS GREW FROM THE 16TH TO 19TH CENTURIES, TYPICALLY TO MASK BALDNESS OR SCARRING FROM DISEASES SUCH AS SYPHILIS.

THE SHAME AND STIGMA ATTACHED TO WIGS AND WEAVES MAINLY AROSE DURING THE 80'S AND 90'S WHEN AFRICAN AMERICAN WOMEN BEGAN DONNING THEM.

TODAY WIGS AND HAIR PIECES ARE MAINSTREAM.

I have witnessed this discrimination. Once, the head of my department stated he holds his nose whenever he is around someone with dreadlocks because they do not wash their hair. Flabbergasted, I corrected him yet realized he likely would never hire someone with locs due to this perception.

Social media has created natural hair influencers, and products that cater to natural hairstyle wearers are as popular as ever. Black women, such as Rhianna and Pat McGrath, are marketing high-quality beauty products to women with deeper and darker skin tones who'd previously been neglected by major beauty brands.

LET ME UPGRADE YOU

When it comes to clothing, there are many adages. "Dress for the job you want, not the one you have," "Dress for Success," "Dress how you want to be addressed," and the list continues. If only we lived in a world where a person's skills and achievements were enough, and appearance was not the focus. Like it or not, the culture of many organizations implies that attire represents one's professionalism towards their work and life.

A great example of how proper apparel can elevate your brand comes from comedian and talk show host Steve Harvey. During an episode of his namesake show, he was coaching a newlywed couple in which the husband was content with dressing casually and the wife was not. He sported a gold mouth grill and chains and did not understand why his wife wanted him to change how he dressed.

In order to get his point across, Steve used a personal example of why listening to his wife may be beneficial to their future. He explained, 'I dressed very different before I married Marjorie Harvey. My pants were this wide; all my shoes matched my hats. I did whatever I wanted to do. But when we were getting married, Marjorie said, 'Steve, where God is going to take you, you have to look different … Put on a more traditional suit … Shorten them pants!'" Steve accepted the wisdom in Marjorie's words and recognized it set him up for greater opportunities in the future. It is a gift when people are placed in our lives to help us reach our fullest potential and elevate our game.

Frequently these conversations are avoided due to fear of causing offense or the belief the advisor is asking someone not to be their authentic self. Re-imagine yourself as an actor. There are multiple roles to play, and to get into character, a costume change may be required. Not all of us have the budget Mr. Harvey has for custom suits and a total wardrobe overhaul. Until you amass your fortune, here are my GOTS rules (no, not *Game of Thrones*) for always looking presentable yet maintaining your personal style.

- Grooming
- Occasion Appropriate

- Tailoring & Fit
- Sheerness

GROOMING: *SO FRESH AND SO CLEAN*

The first rule of fashion or beauty is always start with a clean base. That includes body, hair, nails, teeth, and the actual garments.

- Hair: Recognize there is a difference between unkempt and unruly hair! Whether I am rocking an afro-puff, curly crown, braids, or flowing tresses, I follow these simple rules. No dandruff flakes, tracks, smells, or product build-up. #BigHairDontCare.

- Nails: Should be clean and, especially in business a setting, the length should allow for a firm handshake.

- Body: Freshly showered with non-distracting cologne levels.

Neat and clean does not only apply to your body. This rule also applies to your clothes. I am a rare individual who enjoys ironing. My industrial-sized iron and floor model steamer are invaluable. Preparation is key to looking your best. When I worked a 9-to-5, Sundays were spent preparing my wardrobe for the week, based on the forecast. That included pressing my clothes and setting out the shoes and accessories I planned to wear.

This takes discipline, yet the benefits are tremendous. First, having my clothes ready means the time spent getting ready in the morning is unhurried. Second, while ironing you can inspect your clothes for tears, stains, and even security tags that somehow were left on by the store! I have been a witness and victim of this!

When buying new clothes, take notice of the care instructions. In the past, I spent so much on dry cleaning that it would have been more economical to buy the same item every few months. That was until I became aware of dry cleaners that charge one low price for any garment.

PROPER FIT

One of the most beautiful images in the world is a man in a well-tailored suit. England and Italy are where I am enchanted with the bespoke style of the men. Plus, the accents do not hurt. I advise investing in fine tailoring, even for modestly priced, quality attire. Dressing well is not solely wearing bespoke suits and couture gowns. How you wear your attire impacts how you walk and carry yourself. One cannot comfortably glide across a room like a man in uniform or Denzel Washington if your pants are hanging down to your knees. A stride like Naomi Campbell's cannot be achieved if your dress or bottoms are so tight you barely can place one foot in front of the other. All you can do is slowly and ungracefully shuffle along as you tug on your clothing.

I was a major contributor to the Chicago Mayor Lori Lightfoot meme craze during the 2020 quarantine. During a press conference, the world watched as her petite frame was swallowed by an over-sized suit. Not helping matters was her perfected "death stare." Fortunately, she took the memes in good stride and tweaked her wardrobe.

Another benefit of preparing clothes for the week is giving each outfit a trial run. No bulges, no cups overflowing, and no seams screaming for mercy. A telltale sign of improper fit is constant adjusting.

SHEERNESS

I recommend steering clear of sheer clothes, particularly in the workplace. First, your coworkers should never feel like they have to constantly divert their eyes for fear of seeing something they should not. Secondly, if people are inspecting your outfit, they are not listening to what you are saying.

Inspecting your look for sheerness is required for both men and women. Undershirts for men, and shapewear and slips for women, might save everyone from the sight of nipples, dimples, and forests of body hair. The lighting in part of your home might hinder your ability to determine sheerness, so take a selfie or try to see the outfit in natural light.

OCCASION APPROPRIATE

In my personal and professional opinion, being overdressed is not a real issue. My intent is not to be overdressed, though there have been times when my friends hummed the chorus to "There She Is, Miss America," when I pass. My style is more formal. When the dress code is business casual, I recommend leaning more towards the business side. Clients may visit your office unexpectedly or an after-work event may pop up on your schedule. I am not advocating wearing a three-piece suit in a manufacturing setting. Especially if you are new to a company, ask if they have a manual or discuss the dress code during orientation.

I worked for a company without a dress code because they believed this would attract a younger generation of candidates. Another company had a division in New York with a business casual dress code, yet everyone arrived in designer suits.

The conversation has been raised about whether dress codes are racist or sexist. To prove this point, I would not go as far as comedian Chelsea Handler, who mockingly posted a photo of herself riding a horse topless along with that of a shirtless man with the caption, "If a man posts a photo of his nipples, it's okay, but not a woman?" Personally, I do not have an issue with dress codes; my concerns arise when dress codes are not enforced equitably. My friend Brenda recounted an incident in which her husband was prohibited from a

Chicago supper club because he was not wearing a collared shirt. As they stood nearby deciding their next move, they witnessed some patrons exiting not wearing collared shirts.

Look around. If you are applying for a job at a bank or a fashion house, you would probably have two different suits. This pertains to social gatherings, such as weddings and for companies. Perform the due diligence by asking if there is a dress code if one is not stated. For example, when people show up to all-white parties in something other than all white, they should politely excuse themselves from the event because the organizers were clearly going for certain aesthetics. Organizers should enforce the policy. Unless you are going to your child's school to deliberately embarrass them, leave the house shoes in the house!

* * *

You are *a diamond of the first water* and *flawless, my dear*. Yet all diamonds need polishing. One of the quickest and easiest ways to begin your reincarnation is examining how you carry yourself in clothes. It may be time to retire the old attire!

Travel Noire

"I encourage travel to as many destinations as possible for the sake of education, as well as pleasure."
–Dr. Maya Angelou

Air travel, during its golden age, was prestigious and glamorous; today, it is a most uncivilized affair. Nowadays the boarding process resembles a Black Friday sale at a toy store. Courtesy is thrown out the window as passengers vie for the precious overhead space and remnants of pillows or blankets. Airports and airlines bear some of the blame. Amenities have been greatly reduced and personal space is basically non-existent. Now that air travel has become more accessible due to increased competition among carriers, small queues and elevated experiences are a thing of the past.

Nonetheless, comfort and style do not have to be mutually exclusive. I have been flying the not-so-friendly skies for twenty-plus years. My heart is filled with joy when I see so many adventurous souls living their best lives and experiencing other cultures. Yet I have witnessed a drastic decline in great customer service from the hospitality industry and good manners from the travelers.

Here are some tips for a more graceful voyage.

You'll learn to build relationships with foreigners even if you don't know the language. Additionally, you'll develop stronger cross-cultural sensitivity, self-reliance, and dependability.

BAG LADY, YOU GONE HURT YOUR BACK

I am the queen of packing light. Though I am fashionably dressed throughout my trip, I can easily fit two weeks' worth of clothes into carry-on luggage. Packing light affords me flexibility if travel plans unexpectedly change. I effortlessly glide through airports and avoid the wait, expense, and risk checking bags adds. This may be petty of me, but I refuse to carry travel companions' bags, even though I may have a free hand. If you pack it, you carry it! Or pay to have someone assist with you with your luggage.

Navigating the European train system and the timeworn streets of cities such as Venice, it is best to have as little luggage as possible. Trust me, I learned the hard way. The money spent checking luggage can be spent towards a nice dinner. More times than I care to count, I have seen people frantically rearranging items between bags to avoid paying overweight fees.

- Invest in simple, elegant luggage. IKEA bags are not acceptable. AWAY and T.J. Maxx are great options for finding affordable, yet stylish bags.

- Two pairs of neutral-colored heels are more than adequate. Black, flesh-toned, silver, or gold will suffice.

- Packing light saves room for souvenirs, but do not spend a lot of money on trinkets! I tell my family and friends not to buy me anything when they are on vacation, and I will not buy anything for them. My gift to my friends is the fact I am having a good time and spending my funds on experiences, not knickknacks that will eventually end up in a junk drawer.

ZE PLANE! ZE PLANE!

My age is showing with this *Fantasy Island* quote, but this lighthearted reference relates to the most stressful aspect of exploration: Air Travel. The most critical and stressful legs of any trip is the time spent getting to and leaving your destination, especially if you are doing it by plane. The key to life and travel is avoiding making others uncomfortable. This does not suggest making sacrifices at the expense of your own comfort. Imagine some of the travelers around you have a fear of flying, others are jet-lagged road warriors, and some may be traveling due to a crisis such as the death of a loved one.

As I type this, a friend just shared a viral photo of two people on a commercial aircraft with an aluminum tray of shellfish. If you can move past the smell, can you fathom what those with extreme shellfish allergies must be thinking or experiencing? Imagine if you were a last-minute addition to the flight and had to sit in the middle seat between them.

In interviews, the pair stated they did not receive objections from their fellow passengers, and they felt like stars because people were taking pictures. Likely photos were taken not out of admiration, but to mock them on social media. Furthermore, the lack of criticism does not imply approval or appreciation.

Here are etiquette tips to maintain your peace of mind, while being courteous to others.

The Airport

Check-in - Prior to arriving at the airport, you should research what is acceptable as a carry-on, understand costs for overweight bags, and what must be checked. If you are instructed to adjust your luggage, step aside and allow the ticketing agent to help other customers.

Security - Just because you are cutting it close does not give you the right to cut the line. Keep in mind others ahead of you might be just as crunched for time as you are. Explaining your situation and asking politely to move ahead is appropriate.

Gate - First and foremost, save designated seating for

those in need. In addition, while congregating in the gate area, do not block others from the boarding lane and only board with your respective zone.

Baggage claim - Blocking the conveyor will not result in you getting your bag quicker. Stand aside and allow others enough space to grab their luggage from the carousel.

All Aboard

Overhead storage - Place only <u>one</u> item in an overhead bin closest to your seat until the boarding process is complete. Keep your coats on your lap or hang them backwards on your seat.

Seats - Leaning back the seat, especially for short flights, is not necessary. Are you really that much more comfortable reclining 2-3 inches? If you must, look back and slowly recline and avoid reclining during meal service.

- Stay in your assigned seat, especially for short flights. Being apart from your loved ones for a few hours is not the end of the world, unless there is a child involved. Plus, do not ask someone to sit in a middle seat to convenience you.

- The seat number or entertainment module

designates who the armrest belongs to. It is a kind gesture to allow the middle seat to have two arm rests.

- There is little parents can do about crying infants, so passengers have to grin and bear it. Empathize with them and carry quality earplugs.

- Parents, please keep your children out of the aisles and teach them not to kick the seat in front of them.

- Do not impose your conversations on others. Texts are more than sufficient until you deplane.

- Take visual cues from your neighbor. Putting on eye masks, earbuds, or looking at reading material is a sign they are not in a chatty mood.

- When I take my seat on the plane, I close my eyes, say my "traveling mercies," and then relax. I try to enjoy the time I have to disconnect and become invisible to my seatmates. Remember everyone has a shared goal. Arriving at their destination safely.

ATTIRE

In the April 2014 Version Two of American Airline's *American Way* in-flight magazine, in the customer feedback section, there was an article titled "A Slice of History." A Black American customer had submitted a photograph from the mid-1950s of himself and younger brother as children dressed in what he described as their Sunday best, prior to boarding their flight. As I gazed upon the page of the magazine, I smiled. Six years have passed, yet I vividly recall the photo and the letter and hear my Aunt Ruth's voice echo in my ears, saying Black people used to take pride in how they dressed. Today, people take flight dressed as if they are attending a teenager's sleepover.

As discussed in the previous chapter, *You Wear It Well*, how you dress may influence the quality of service you receive. I am not condoning this yet recognize the society in which we live passes judgment on appearance. Here are my basic recommendations:

- All black and dark colors are always chic and camouflage travel grime. My long-sleeve maxi dress with pockets is my go-to travel uniform.

- A neck scarf can add an elegant pop of color and provide warmth on the flight or train, plus play double duty as a hairstyle protector on overnight flights.

- I admire people who wear stilettos throughout airport terminals, though I have yet to see someone do it effortlessly. Stylish flats will do fine.

- Wearing minimum jewelry at the airport allows you to breeze through security. You do not want to run the risk of losing these valuables during security screening. A pair of small studs and wedding ring is adequate.

- No one wants to arrive at their destination with bedhead; however, wearing hair bonnets or du-rags in the airport is not recommended. For long-haul flights, wait until the cabin lights are dimmed to don your protective hair accessories.

What you wear on the flight is not the only consideration. Perform research on the customs and restrictions of the place you are visiting. For example, the norms on the beaches of Brazil are not the same as those on the streets of Egypt. I visited temples in Thailand where I was asked to cover my shoulders and mosques in Abu Dhabi and Jordan, where I was provided with material to cover my head. I always graciously comply. Though you may hold strong beliefs that your attire is a form of freedom of expression, remember you are a "guest" in another country. Please abide by and respect the local traditions because not doing so is inconsiderate. It could also be dangerous if you stick out like a sore thumb or break a local law.

Additional Tips:

- Know the people you are traveling with to avoid embarrassing conflicts. Ironically, those closest to you may not be the best travel companions.

- Travel sophistication is going other places without the expectation it will be the same as where you just left. Respect other cultures and recognize standards and the ways of life are not the same.

- Research the host country to mitigate offending its citizens. Learn a few key phrases, major historical events, and current affairs. Should I shake hands, bow, or kiss on the cheek? Do I offer to take off my shoes? Should I tip?

- Even now you might be the only person of color this person will meet so represent the culture well. In 2010, I traveled to Qingdao, China, for work. In a city of seven million people, I only saw one other Black person in more than two weeks I was there.

- Travel shaming on social media is impolite. Posting that people need to get out of their element and travel more is inconsiderate. If someone is more comfortable only traveling domestically or repeating the same trip, that is his or her prerogative. Keep the judgment to yourself.

A House Is A Home

"The ache for home lives in all of us, the safe place where we can go as we are and not be questioned."
–Dr. Maya Angelou

It is equally a great honor to be an invited houseguest or play host to a cherished guest. Though the host is displaying great generosity, having people in their space can still be exhausting. For an introvert like myself, this especially rings true. "White Glove Service" for my guests requires me to clean before, during, and after their visit; in addition to providing my undivided attention. According to *Psychology Today*, "houseguests are stressful to the extent that they disrupt our routines and usurp the high amount of control we normally enjoy in this personal territory."[11]

Though hosting guests may be exhausting, I, admittedly, make a great houseguest. At a minimum, I use the "Leave No Trace" methodology, or add value by

---

[11] *Psychology Today*: "The Trouble With Houseguests" by Shawn M. Burn, Ph.D

finding a home organization project that will benefit the host. The bed must be made, suitcase tucked away in the closet or under the bed, towels neatly hung, and toiletries placed under the sink.

What can be done to ensure guests feel welcome and hosts are not in need of a vacation from their houseguests? Here are some tried and true recommendations.

HOSTESS WITH THE MOSTEST

- Confirm (and re-confirm) the details of your guest's stay well in advance of their arrival. Find out the dates of their arrival and departure and special needs (e.g., pick-up from the airport, access to your car, extra key).

- At a minimum, ensure there is a dedicated, tidy sleeping space and clean linens for your guests.

- Basic nourishment such as fruit and crackers should be available. In addition, map out a clear dining plan and make necessary reservations. Typically, I do not stock up on groceries prior to having guests because many times they want to go out to enjoy the culinary scene in Chicago. However, if your home is in a remote location, I would suggest asking them for a list of grocery items or having enough for a continental breakfast and midday snack.

- Do not be offended if your guests have other plans with people they know in the city. Enjoy the quiet time and freshen up the house while they are away.

BE MY GUEST

- Leave no trace. All attempts should be made to leave the residence exactly as you found it or better.

- Remember you are not at an all-inclusive hotel and the hosts are not there to wait on you hand and foot. Clean up after yourself.

- Though your host may say you are welcome to everything in the house, be wary of popping open the expensive champagne you found in the fridge. It may have sentimental value.

- If the bar or snack cabinet is depleted by the end of your stay, make a store run to replace the items or provide the host with a gift certificate.

- Bring your own toiletries.

- If it is a non-smoking household, I suggest taking a short walk to have your smoke break. This prevents the smoke smell from blowing back into the house and allows you to air out before coming back in.

- Mix & mingle: The home of a friend or acquaintance is not an Airbnb! It is not optional to interact with the host and come and go as you choose. If you have other obligations during your stay, make your host aware ahead of time, so they will not plan anything during that time.

- Mind your business: Please do not snoop in drawers, cabinets, or closed rooms.

- Do not invite others over to the home, without explicit permission from the homeowner.

- Dress appropriately: Please cover yourself (e.g. no sexy or revealing sleepwear). No "bouncing" around, especially if your host's significant other is present.

- Refrain from posting photos or details about their home on social media. Not everyone wants the world to know what they have or where they live.

- Know when to leave: As the saying goes, "Guests, like fish, begin to smell after three days," especially if quarters are cramped.

- Leave a thank you: Plan and leave a handwritten thank you card prior to your departure, in addition to taking the host to dinner during your stay.

LOVE THY NEIGHBOR

Only a rarefied population of the world do not have neighbors. We spend our lives being neighbors whether you live in a dorm, house, or apartment. As I am typing this, I am at a friend's apartment where her neighbor is using his garage as an art studio, resulting in the hallways reeking of the chemical smell of a nail salon. Not only have I been a lifelong neighbor; I have been a landlord who had to deal with tenants not respecting my property or our contractual agreement.

Unwritten rules to follow in order to live in a state of grace with "thy neighbor:"

- Maintain your property so that it does not impact the property value of others. I recall a friend saying that her husband's maintenance of the lawn was lacking; therefore, the couple next door cut their grass when they were in the process of selling their home. If time or physical constraints are the reason you cannot preserve your landscape, then find a teen from the neighborhood or a contractor to do it for you. In addition, clean up after using common spaces, including not leaving behind junk mail.

- Let the volume from activities mirror the sun. Everyone enjoys a good house party from time to time. If your neighbors are not included in the festivities, make sure to inform them that noise and traffic will increase during a specified time frame. A bottle of wine or cookies goes a long way in building goodwill with your neighbors.

- I have done my fair share of condo and apartment living. Therefore, I understand the challenges of shared walls and common spaces, such as staring at the ceiling while another resident constantly drops weights in the gym or look on in dismay as residents move via the passenger elevators versus properly scheduling the freight elevator. For condominium owners and renters, learn the official home association or building rules, then follow them. If others are not abiding by the rules, document and inform management to avoid direct conflict with those you must live with. In addition, I recommend attending board meetings in order to voice your concerns and be conscious of current affairs.

- As the famous show business quotes goes "never work with children and animals," though they are dearly loved, the same can be said about living with or near them. Though beyond their control, their trail of chaos can negatively impact your neighbors. Options: Send your fur baby to obedience school or buy your neighbors some good earplugs or a white noise machine as you explore moving.

Commencement

*"If a person does not invent herself, she will be
invented. So, to be bodacious enough to invent
ourselves is wise."*
–Dr. Maya Angelou

Change can be difficult and scary, yet if there is
no change, there is no growth. Have you
looked through old photos, then wondered,
"What was I thinking?" Whether it was bad fashion,
relationships, or job choices, we all have judged our past.
Going forward, choose the change you want to see in
your life. Do not allow circumstances or the surrounding
environment to force you into making a decision.

*"Our crown has already been bought and paid for.
All we have to do is wear it."* This quote by the masterful
Mr. James Baldwin is so poignant because, in my
training to become an etiquette instructor, it was
explained that, among the aristocracy, tiaras are only
inherited, never bought. The crown I wear has been
passed down to me by all the wise elders and
contemporaries who have paved the way, so I can hold
my head up with grace. The village is here to ensure you

have all the tools you need to make sure your crown is tightly secured.

Though I am easy prey for British period dramas, such as *Downton Abbey, Sandition,* and *The Duchess,* I believe one does not have to be "high born" to be a gentlewoman or gentleman. The *Merriam-Webster's Dictionary* defines a gentlewoman as "a woman of refined manners or good breeding," and a gentleman as "a chivalrous, courteous, or honorable man." It does not state one must be part of a family with titles, highly educated, or of great wealth.

To reinvent yourself or solidify your skills as a gentleman or gentlewomen, here are the "Lucky 13" essentials for your toolkit.

1. A witty comeback (or redirection) for rude or intrusive questions.

2. A genuine laugh. To complement your dazzling smile and your witty comeback.

3. A cause or ideal that benefits others that is very dear to your heart. Plus, it can be used as a tool to deflect intrusive questions or a conversation starter.

4. Honest and reliable friends. Even those of us who believe we are so evolved have blinders. That is when direct feedback from friends is most valuable.

5. A vacation on the books. It does not have to be somewhere exotic or expensive. Rent a car for a day trip to unexplored or familiar territory. For example, travel to the town where you can trace your family's roots. Or visit the small restaurant you saw on a cooking show.

6. A flattering pair of sunglasses for those all-nighters. Otherwise, stock up on eye drops.

7. A rainy-day fund. Use an app to squirrel away money with little effort.

8. Comfortable, yet stylish shoes. I do not know which is more painful—having sore, swollen feet or watching someone else with aching feet attempting to walk-in ill-fitting shoes.

9. Good posture. Take adult ballet lessons, sit with a pillow propped behind you, or go old school by balancing a book on your head. Recently, I visited Ghana and the sight of women balancing objects of all sizes on their head was quite striking. They had the bearing of queens due to their perfect posture and graceful gait. Keep in mind walking while looking down at your phone is not alluring!

10. Breath Mints: Avoid chewing gum in the presence of others because, at times, we are not

aware we are smacking, or you might have a mortifying moment like I did when my gum come fell out of my mouth while meeting with my vice-president.

11. Legible handwriting. Purchase handwriting or calligraphy exercise guides for your practice. Your thank you notes will be utterly sublime!

12. Handkerchiefs: Monogrammed versions are best, and tissues are a good secondary option as long as they do not leave a trail of lint.

13. Dinnerware: Have, at least, one place setting of china that you use daily. It does not have to be expensive. Flea markets and thrift stores are goldmines for these items.

* * *

Dear Friend,

Congratulations on embarking on or continuing your genteel journey towards a more graceful and grace-filled life. Words cannot express how grateful and humbled I am that you read this book. I truly hope you enjoyed this guide on social graces as seen from a modern, Black American point of view. Plus, Dr. Maya Angelou's quotes sublimely capture all aspects of a graceful life! I highly recommend exploring her works.

Be mindful that proper etiquette and good manners

are just as important today as they have been for centuries. Though I would like this handbook to be as comprehensive as possible, it cannot cover everything. Etiquette is continually evolving; therefore, social graces should not be left to chance. Stay current by studying and practicing.

Remember:

- *Do not be defined by your circumstances. Everyone has the capacity to become a gentleman or gentlewoman, regardless of his or her background.*

- *Be clear on what you value and the type of image you want to project.*

- *Practice. Learn the rules and fill your toolkit with the proper techniques.*

I look forward to seeing you shape society into a kinder and more respectful world.

Sincerely,
Nicole

Acknowledgments

A special thanks to my book accountability buddies, amateur editors, queens, and sister-friends, Dr. Judith C. Davis, Dana Hardy, Jessica Simmons, and Nicole Renee Robinson. Your love and support are invaluable. Because of you, I can soar high, knowing I have a soft place to land.

For those who came before me, I thank and honor you for your sacrifices, which have allowed me to find and live my purpose.

Special thanks to my village of loved ones and friends who support me no matter what! Much love and respect to all of you!

"A man's manners are a mirror in which he shows his portrait." —Johann Wolfgang von Goethe, *Maxims and Reflections*

About the Author

 Nicole Reed is an international social & business etiquette and ethics expert. She holds a degree in Finance with a History Minor, and has over twenty years of global business compliance, finance, and customer service experience. In London, she completed her etiquette and protocol studies with the highest honors at The English Manner, which was founded by a former member of The Royal Household of Her Majesty the Queen and taught by the world's leading experts.

You can connect with me on:

https://www.reednwright.com
https://twitter.com/Reed_N_Wright
https://www.facebook.com/EtiquetteAndEthics
https://www.instagram.com/reednwright

CPSIA information can be obtained
at www.ICGtesting.com
Printed in the USA
BVHW061354030222
627977BV00017B/592

9 781953 307989